Bunty Avieson worked for twenty years as a journalist on newspapers and magazines in Australia and Britain. She was Editor of *Woman's Day* and Editorial Director of *New, Idea*, winning three Magazine Publishers Association Awards. She is also a Williamson Fellow (1999).

In 2000 Bunty took up fiction writing full time. Her first novel, *Apartment 255*, won two Ned Kelly Crime Writing Awards and has been translated into German and Japanese. She has written two other novels, *The Affair* and *The Wrong Door*.

Bunty lives with her partner and daughter, dividing her time between Sydney and India.

buntyavieson@bigpond.com

Also by Bunty Avieson

Apartment 255
The Affair
The Wrong Door

A BABY IN A BACKPACK TO BHUTAN

An Australian family in the
Land of the Thunder Dragon

BUNTY AVIESON

MACMILLAN
Pan Macmillan Australia

First published 2004 in Macmillan by Pan Macmillan Australia Pty Limited
St Martins Tower, 31 Market Street, Sydney

National Library of Australia
Cataloguing-in-Publication data:

Avieson, Bunty.
A baby in a backpack to Bhutan: An Australian family
in the Land of the Thunder Dragon.

ISBN 1 40503582 X.

1. Avieson, Bunty - Journeys - Bhutan. 2. Australians -
Bhutan - Biography. 3. Bhutan - Description and travel.
4. Bhutan - Social life and customs. I. Title.

915.498

Papers used by Pan Macmillan Australia Pty Ltd are natural, recyclable
products made from wood grown in sustainable forests. The manufacturing
processes conform to the environmental regulations of the country of origin.

Typeset in 13 pt Granjon by Midland Typesetters
Map by Laurie Whiddon
Printed in Australia by McPherson's Printing Group

This is dedicated with much love and affection to those luminous women of Taba – Karma Yangki, Phuntsho Wangmo, Karma Chokyi and Wesel Wangmo.

And to Kathryn Rose – you make everything so much fun.

Contents

Acknowledgements

With heartfelt thanks to Dzongsar Khyentse Rinpoche and all his monks at Bir, Pema Wangchuk and the Siddhartha's Intent household in Delhi, Sogyal Rinpoche, Mani Dorji and Tenzin Wangdi in Thimphu, Douglas Mills for his Tibetan translations, Linda Smith, Sandra Lee, Tom Gilliatt, Karen Penning, Sharon Metzl, Selwa Anthony and the very gorgeous Mal Watson.

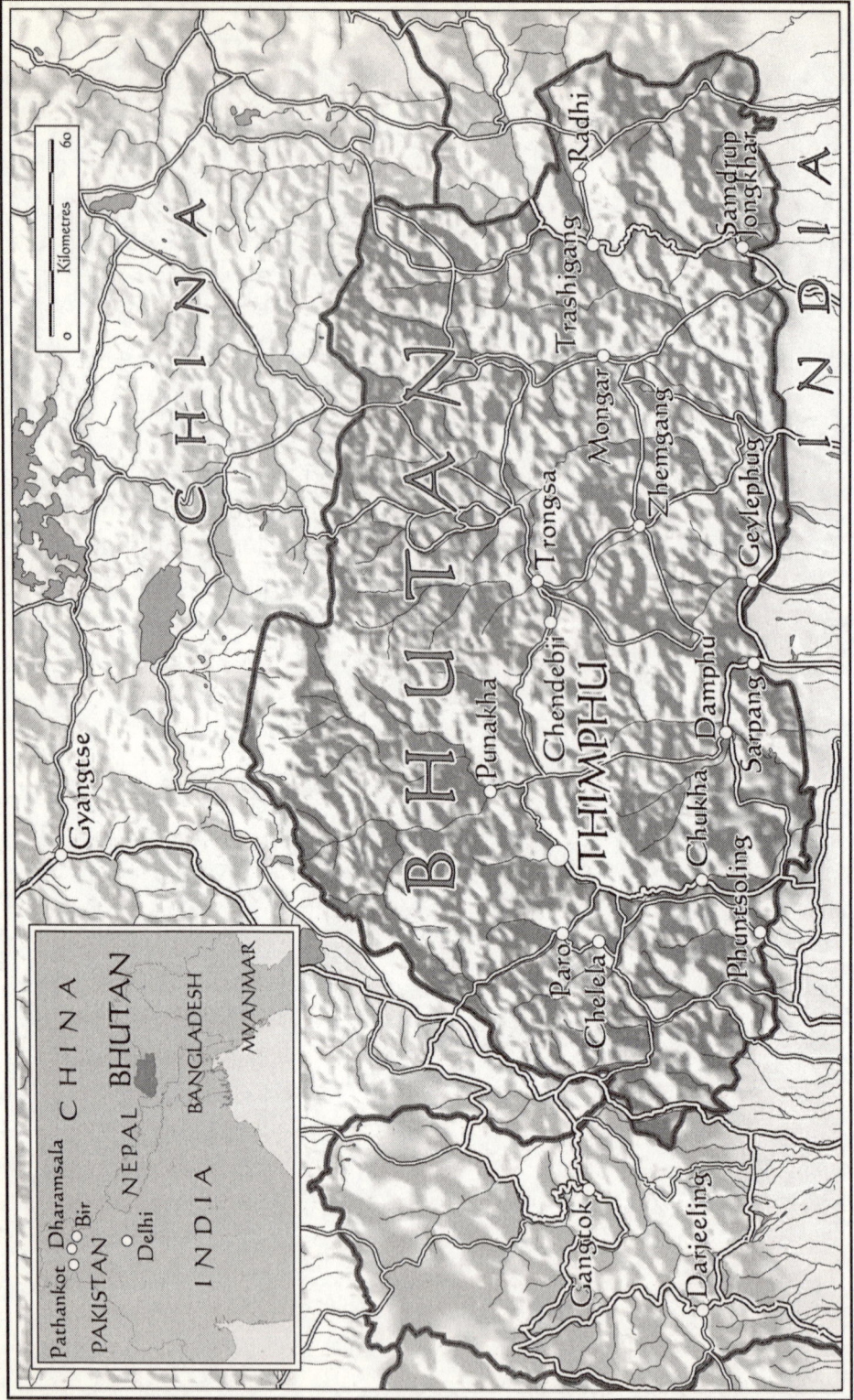

CHINA

Gyangtse

BHUTAN

THIMPHU

Radhi

Trashigang

Samdrup
Jongkhar

Mongar

Zhemgang

Trongsa

Chendebji

Gevlephug

Punakha

Damphu

Chukha

Sarpang

Paro

Chelela

Phuntsoling

INDIA

Gangtok

Darjeeling

Prologue

THIMPHU, BHUTAN

2 AUGUST 2003

It's 5 pm on a Saturday afternoon. Monsoon rains are hammering on the roof of the marquee, the air is steamy and I'm quietly drowning in sweat inside my *kira*, a thick, heavy piece of woven cloth that is so tightly wrapped around me I can hardly breathe. In front of me sit the Queens of Bhutan, four elegant and beautiful sisters who are all married to the country's ruler, the Dragon King.

Beside me, my partner Mal is exhausted and relieved. The movie he produced has just had its world premiere, here in Thimphu, Bhutan's tiny capital. *Travellers & Magicians* has been given the royal nod and at this genteel post-premiere reception he can finally relax.

Cavorting happily in the rain in front of the royal entourage is our eighteen-month-old daughter Kathryn, stumbling about on the grass in her miniature *kira*. It is the country's national costume, which by law the Bhutanese women must wear, and out of respect, we do also. While she looks cute, I look like a round multicoloured keg.

One of the Queens turns her head and exchanges pleasantries

with Mal and me. It is one of the few occasions that we can look Her Majesty in the eye without being considered rude.

In this unique little kingdom nestled in the Himalayas, royal protocol normally forbids such intimacy. I have heard many funny stories of drivers who, spotting a royal car on the road ahead, have driven into fields and rice paddies as they dutifully lowered their gaze. The reverence the people feel for their first family is extraordinary. The Royals are considered a national treasure.

The King has decreed that Gross National Happiness is more important than Gross National Product. And that's how his people live. For many, life is a struggle, yet they remain remarkably content and happy. It is a little pocket of sanity in a world gone mad.

It seems like just a minute ago that I was Editorial Director of an Australian weekly women's magazine. It was a crazy, hyper world of celebrity gossip and glamour, big money and even bigger egos. And I loved every mad minute of it.

Interrupting my thoughts, a handsome waiter with feline eyes and angular cheekbones (and wearing what looks suspiciously like an orange tartan dressing gown) offers me another yak hors d'oeuvre. The Queen engages me in polite conversation, saying kind things about my daughter as she frolics in front of us, wet but happy.

This is about as far away from that Sydney magazine office – and all the corporate brouhaha that went with it – as I could possibly get without actually leaving the planet. By some fortunate set of circumstances that I never saw coming and wouldn't have dared even imagine, I have arrived here, at this enchanting moment, in Shangri-la.

I

A New Life

MAY 2000

I meet Malcolm Watson at an inner-city cafe in Sydney on a blind date. Sort of. Mal lives mostly in India but is currently home visiting his family. He works as an architect on projects for an international charitable organisation and was co-producer of the delightful multi-award-winning movie *The Cup* – about soccer-mad monks in a Tibetan monastery in India. A friend, aware of my growing interest in Buddhism, thinks I might find him helpful and so she organises dinner at her place. Half an hour before we are due, she phones to say she's ill and will have to postpone. I suggest she gives Mal my number and that the two of us can go out somewhere for dinner. She phones back to say he's shy and would rather we rescheduled. Used to running my personal life like my professional life, I take down his number and phone him.

'I know you're free for dinner, well so am I. How about it?'

He has the grace to say yes.

I choose an inexpensive Nepalese restaurant in the inner

city, figuring it's probably the sort of place he will like. I arrive on time and wait, the only person in the room, watching the door for someone with a beard and sandals, maybe beads, and possibly smelling of incense.

Mal is nothing like the hippy I am expecting. He is clean shaven, conservatively dressed in jeans and an open-neck shirt, and wears leather shoes with laces. Arriving at my table, he takes one look around the deserted restaurant and says he knows a much better place – a groovy Italian bistro in Darlinghurst.

We decamp there and I trot out all my questions about Buddhism – karma, reincarnate lamas, personal gurus and so on – all the things I just can't get my Anglican-educated head around. He doesn't directly answer a single one. I come at him from five different ways which, as a journalist, I'm used to doing. He sidesteps them all so neatly that I don't even realise until we are two steps past.

Dinner is pleasant enough anyway and we agree to meet for lunch the following Saturday. This time I avoid all the vegetarian haunts of inner Sydney and suggest a little spot overlooking a park. We move from the restaurant to my apartment and talk non-stop for sixteen hours, about anything and everything. He leaves at 5 am just as the sun is rising, and we shake hands, rather formally, at my front door. It's only as I watch him walk up the driveway that I realise he still hasn't answered any of my questions about his personal Buddhist path.

I think he's funny, pretty laidback, and probably the most fascinating man I've ever met. Even after so much talk, I feel like we haven't finished our conversation. He feels the same and delays his return to India. We see each other every evening for the next ten days.

I'd been planning a two-week holiday in America with friends. Mal says, 'Cancel that, come to India. I'll show you around.' May is such a lovely time of year to see the country, he tells me.

Of course! Why not? I've known you for a nanosecond.

I'm astounded that I say yes. But three weeks after meeting Mal, I'm in the doctor's office getting vaccinations.

'Where are you going?' asks the Indian cabbie who drives me to Sydney Airport.

'Delhi.'

'You're crazy! No-one goes to Delhi in May – it's the hottest time of the year. People *leave* Delhi. I'm from Delhi and tomorrow I'm coming back to the airport to pick up my mother. Every year at this time she comes to Sydney to get away from the heat . . .'

I decide this is further proof that all men lie during courtship.

❋

When I get off the plane amid the chaos of Delhi Airport, my courage deserts me – what the hell am I doing here, meeting a man I hardly know? I stand in limbo at the customs gate. Outside is a sea of faces and colour and noise. I can't go back and my feet just won't propel me forward. I'm suddenly very embarrassed and shy. What if he isn't out there . . . worse still, what if he is? Will I even recognise him?

People push past me, eager to get to their families, and are absorbed into the crush of bodies ringing the customs exit. My high-pressure world of magazine publishing suddenly seems very sane. I would rather be facing manic deadlines and hysterical publicists than get sucked into this frightening vortex.

With great reluctance I push my trolley through the gates and stop, mesmerised by all the faces. It appears as if the whole population of Delhi is crowded into the arrivals hall. But I'm lucky. At just under two metres, Mal stands head and shoulders above the rest. He's also blond, which is enormously helpful. I make my way to him and he wraps me in a bear hug. I think it just might be okay.

3

Delhi is even worse than the driver had predicted. I feel like I'm standing at the door of an open pizza oven. By day the temperature reaches an unbearable 47 degrees Celsius; at night it drops down to a still unbearable 30 degrees. I can't breathe. I have no energy. The moment I walk outside the air-conditioned hotel I'm drenched with rivulets of sweat on my back, my arms and in my eyes.

The people of the city limp through May and June in a kind of mindless stupor. Rickshaw drivers don't work in the middle of the day but instead take a nap by the side of the road at the street intersections. Anyone who can afford to flees the city, mostly heading for the hills. Mal suggests we do the same.

※

We catch an overnight train to Bir, a Tibetan refugee settlement of about 3000 people nestled in the foothills of the Himalayas, north of Delhi. This is where Mal spends most of his time while in India.

Though born in Sydney, Mal has worked for Dzongsar Khyentse Rinpoche and his charitable organisation Siddhartha's Intent for more than a decade, overseeing the building of retreat centres and monasteries in Canada, India and Bhutan as well as co-producing Rinpoche's 1999 film *The Cup*. The movie was made here in Bir, and Mal continues to be involved in an ongoing project designing various monastery buildings for Rinpoche.

Bir is truly the most magical place, although it shares the frustrations of any city in India – intermittent electricity, garbage and plastic bags strangling the waterways, inadequate sanitation, stray diseased dogs that fight and bark all night, poor telecommunications, corrupt Indian officials, desperate poverty, heat and disease.

But despite all the chaos, Bir exists as a unique little oasis of beauty and harmony.

We stay at Rinpoche's house, the Khyentse *labrang*. Mal's 'boss', Dzongsar Khyentse Rinpoche, is a Buddhist lama who travels the world teaching and in his spare time wrote and directed *The Cup*. In Bir he has a much-respected institute for 350 monks and tucked behind it is Khyentse *labrang*, which is his home and personal headquarters when he is here.

Bir is one of the parcels of land the Indian Government has leased to Tibet's government-in-exile for a period of ninety-nine years. While much of the western world argues about refugees and houses immigrants in detention camps, India, despite its own staggering poverty, has made welcome the Tibetans fleeing Chinese occupation, many of whom walked over harsh snow-covered terrain, sometimes for three months or more, to get here. More than 120 000 Tibetans have made it safely to India, Nepal and Bhutan since 1959. That was the year that their spiritual and political leader His Holiness the Dalai Lama moved out, arriving half-dead at the Indian border. Each year more Tibetans attempt the same hazardous journey. They are sent to refugee camps, where they receive health care, before being relocated to Tibetan townships such as Bir.

There are two different townships, known locally as Indian Bir (up the hill), which has a few Indian-run shops, and a few kilometres away is the Tibetan settlement known simply as Bir. The community is made up of monks and families as well as some Indians running their businesses side by side with the Tibetans. In the main street of Bir an Indian man has a shed-shop, made from corrugated iron. He sells mostly the same grocery items as the Tibetan man opposite, and while the two business rivals wait for customers, they happily play cards together on the ground.

There are two telephone shops at either end of the main street, one run by some young Tibetans, the other by a deaf-mute Indian, whose shop is always full of monks calling family around the country or in Tibet and Bhutan. When we need to call home, this is where we come. We take our place in the queue and when it's our turn, we write the phone number on a

Siddharth as intent.org

piece of paper and pass it across the counter to the proprietor. Then we wait in a small booth for the phone to ring. It seems incongruous that someone who can neither hear nor speak is running a telephone shop. It seems even stranger when I discover that the Indian Government, as part of a program to help the disabled, assisted with finance to set up his business.

He is cheerful and efficient, and also runs a lucrative sideline in photocopying. In this he has no competition. Such is his attention to detail that all the monks bring him their *pecha* (horizontal Tibetan books) to copy. These are prayer books and esoteric Buddhist texts, about thirty-by-ten centimetres in size, and made up of between 100 and 500 loose-leaf pages. While he doesn't understand a word of the ornate Tibetan script, he is precise and methodical, perfectly reproducing entire books in a matter of hours.

※

Each evening at dusk we join the local community on 'the walk'. It is a stretch of road that leads out of the main township, winding through tea plantations, past traditional Himachali mudbrick homes, to the river. In the north-east the land creeps slowly higher then rises dramatically to the mountains, and above that the snow-capped Himalayas. Many adventurous westerners come here to hang-glide, taking off from those mountaintops and soaring above the valley alongside the kites, massive eagle-like birds native to this area.

To the west the land slopes gently down the Kangra Valley. As the sun sets, the dust turns it a brilliant red and you are able to look directly at it with the naked eye. There is so much sky and space that the sun seems to take ages to sink down to the horizon, only to suddenly and dramatically drop out of view. It is an awesome sight that always draws a crowd, particularly on Sundays.

Bir has four monasteries, representing different lineages or schools of Tibetan Buddhism. For six days a week the monks' intense study schedule starts around 4 am and can finish at 8 pm or later, so Sunday nights are one of the few opportunities for them to relax and be sociable.

We see them everywhere along the road, their maroon robes draped around their waist and slung over one shoulder. Most are dapper and carry themselves with great pride, looking learned and dignified like Roman senators, only in dark red, not white. Some look scruffy, as if they slept in their clothes. Others, particularly the young ones, are mischievous as they run around teasing and chasing each other or kicking a soccer ball. Some hold hands as they walk together. It has no romantic connotations, Mal assures me after one monk, an old friend, grabs his hand and walks with us for a few hundred metres.

As well as the monks, the road is always abuzz with people strolling, chatting, admiring the sunset, looking for a good vantage point for the final act or heading for their favourite spot. Tibetan women, demure in their *chuba*s, their pinafore-style national dress, knit and gossip as they walk, children running around their legs. The occasional cow meanders past, used to having right of way on every road in India. Everyone, it seems, comes out to watch the sunset, enjoy the waning day and socialise.

It is here that Mal brings me to continue our conversation and courtship. The man's got class. It is a divine idyll of unsurpassed beauty and simplicity. He buys two bottles of Coke from a shop along the way and points out a grassy patch, where we sit down to enjoy the passing parade.

For the Indian women in the fields, this is the busiest part of their day and they are bent double carrying huge cane baskets on their back as they pick the young tea shoots, the best part of the bush. Dressed in their colourful saris they smile and chat as they work, sometimes stopping to stare at Mal and me, curious but friendly. In another field a young man manoeuvres a bull and wooden plough over the dirt, which is full of hard clumps of clay. It looks exhausting.

When darkness falls everyone makes their way back to their

homes for dinner. As Mal and I walk back to the *labrang*, alongside the high brick walls of Dzongsar Institute, the air erupts with the ferocious noise of hundreds of men yelling and screaming. It sounds to me like all 350 monks are involved in the most aggressive and bloody of footy matches. Mal finds that idea highly amusing. He takes my hand and leads me through the dark to an unlocked back gate. I'm a little shocked that we're going in there – inside the monastery. Mal obviously knows his way around, which I find only partly reassuring.

'Is this okay?' I ask. 'Me being a woman, I mean?'

He finds this even funnier and assures me the monks won't all go gaga at the sight of my unbridled womanliness.

We walk down some stairs, up a path, around a bend and out onto a grassed courtyard overlooking a huge floodlit quadrangle. The sight almost beggars belief and it takes me ages to make sense of what I'm seeing. The area is crowded with hundreds of monks yelling and berating each other, their faces fierce and animated, hands waving about wildly, even threateningly, while others stand by listening, frowning or sometimes laughing and cheering. It is bedlam, a cacophony of noise. I'm stupefied. What on earth is going on?

Conversation is impossible in the midst of so much sound, but gradually I realise there is some sort of order to what is happening. The monks are sitting or crouching in circles of up to ten men, with occasional pairs. In the centre of each circle are two men, one standing and yelling at the other, clapping his hands as he stands over his crouching opponent. The clapping isn't applause. It's aggressive and intimidatory as the monk slaps one hand over the other, making the palms connect loudly. In some of the circles the opponent is physically cowering. It's an arresting sight that reminds me of gladiator movies where groups of bare-chested men stand around cheering and egging the fighters on as they wrestle each other to the ground.

I find out later that the monks were debating, testing themselves against each other and honing their skills of philo-sophical thought and analysis. This institute is renowned throughout the subcontinent for the erudition and sharp intellect of its students. With its nine-year degree course for a masters of philosophy, Dzongsar produces some of the most skilled debaters of Buddhist philosophy.

The debates are conducted with one monk expounding his theory. Every time he makes a point, he swipes his hand across his palm, the physical equivalent of 'so be it'. The opponent listens respectfully, then when it's his turn, he leaps to his feet and pursues those lines of thought, while onlookers indicate their approval or disapproval. The monks love this form of word play and dance of ideas. Even Tibetan laypeople, while speaking the language, cannot necessarily follow the abstract issues being discussed.

Debating competitions are held throughout the year at various monasteries across India where the very best pit their wits against each other. Noise and energy are features of Tibetan education at all levels. In the schools the children learn by memorisation and recitation – the more voice they give, the more they please their teacher.

Walking past monasteries we hear the young boys, some whose voices have not yet broken, yelling the Tibetan prayers, playfully competing with each other to be loudest. We don't understand a word but their enthusiasm is evident and I find myself smiling along.

✳

The next morning Mal takes me into the kitchen of Dzongsar Institute where meals are prepared for the 350 monks. It is about the size of my own small kitchen back in Sydney, and not nearly as well equipped.

Mal is designing a new kitchen for the institute and updates the monk, who is the head chef and speaks good English, on when the fittings will arrive and what to expect. The monk can hardly believe his ears. What Mal describes is utter luxury.

He has ordered six enormous 250-litre steel pots that will be connected to a huge steam generator in the basement. Each pot has a side lever so that one monk can effortlessly pour the contents – rice, *dhal*, tea and whatever meat or vegetable dish is being prepared that day – into smaller steel pots, which come with a trolley to deliver them to the table. The trolleys will perfectly match the height of three gas burners.

The monk's eyes grow larger and larger.

To top it all off there'll be an oven big enough to steam hundreds of *momo*s at a time. These are the traditional dough dumplings filled with meat or vegetables, a bit like dim sims only much tastier.

All of this is being made by a company in Bangalore, south India, a five-day drive away by truck. When it is finished the monk and his four helpers will move from a gas ring in a lean-to with no running water, to a custom-designed industrial kitchen. Their delight is infectious and we leave with their laughter ringing in our ears.

❋

In every possible way Bir is a world away from my life. Lovely to visit but all too soon the two weeks are up and it's time to go home. Back to my job at *New Idea* and circulation figures, celebrity dramas and battles for stories. And time to say goodbye to Mal.

A few weeks after returning home Mal suddenly appears on my doorstep in Sydney. Just wanted to say hi, he says. Can only stay five days. We both know it's serious. We don't even think about the complications our lives might offer.

A month later we both have business in Europe. It seems the universe is being helpful and we make the most of it, managing to combine our trips. Mal meets me in London for my appointments, then I travel with him to Motovun, a tiny medieval town in Croatia, where he is presenting *The Cup* at a four-day film festival.

Friends are more than a little alarmed that suddenly not

only am I out of the office – enough of a shock in itself – but I'm wandering the world, going to obscure places with a man they just can't get a handle on. One friend emails me because she's heard that I'm going out with an Indian refrigerator repairman. Another tells me she too wants to go to India and give out kitchens to the poor. They don't understand anything about this enigmatic man who has stolen my heart.

'Yes, but what does he *do*?' they ask.

'He works for a Bhutanese lama.'

'You've gone mad.'

Maybe.

At the same time that my personal life is taking such an unexpected and happy turn, in the most glorious piece of synchronicity, a wonderful opportunity opens up profes-sionally.

I come home from Motovun to news from literary agent Selwa Anthony that the half-finished manuscript for a novel, which I had slipped into her handbag at a work lunch one day, has been picked up by a major publishing house. They don't just like it, they are offering an advance to finish it and write a second one.

The world really has gone mad. Suddenly I'm being offered a career beyond magazines, one I have dreamed of since I was a child, one that I can do while travelling the world with a certain six-foot-two man with no fixed address but a very fancy Italian coffee machine. I tell my boss I quit. I'm off to write books. He gives me a sideways look, and says he'll give me six months' paid leave, enough time to get this madness out of my system.

Even better – I'm being offered a safety net. I'm not so blinded by love that I don't realise I'm throwing away a per-fectly good, well-paying career for the vagaries of life as a writer on the road, and with a man I have known just four months. I'm not even sure I can finish the book. Writing it at home for fun is one thing, but turning it into a book for publi-cation, to be read by other people . . . oh lordy.

But how will I ever know if I don't give it a try, I tell myself. Publishing houses don't just hand out book contracts every day, and such an opportunity may never come again.

※

Three weeks later, while the rest of the world is flying into Sydney for the Olympic Games, I catch one of the empty aeroplanes out, to join Mal in Canada where he's wearing his architect's cap and working just outside Vancouver. A more dramatic contrast to the world of magazines I can't imagine.

The Sea to Sky Retreat Center comprises a number of timber cabins set on forty acres of wild, pristine Canadian wilderness. The centre is built around the vast mirror-like Daisy Lake. In the distance loom the snow-covered mountains of Whistler and Blackcomb.

There are no telephones, TV, radio or newspapers, not even a whole lot of conversation as the few other people that are here are on silent retreat.

While they study and do their meditations in their quarters and Mal plays lumberjack outside, I sit in a cosy cabin, my mind back in my Sydney apartment where my book is set. We all meet up for a quiet lunch then go our separate ways again until dinnertime.

It is the perfect way to disengage from magazines and throw myself into writing.

※

After a few months Mal has to be back in Bir to oversee the installation of the new kitchen so we return to India. It is January and bitterly cold. And quiet. Most of the Tibetans are away selling their hand-knitted woolly jumpers and the monks are on holiday. There's just a handful of people left behind, the stray dogs and us.

The truck with the kitchen fittings doesn't arrive and each

day brings a new, more outrageous story. It's lost somewhere in the middle of India, says the company manager by telephone from Bangalore. 'We found the vehicle but the driver got drunk and wandered off' is the next excuse. And: 'The truck hit a pothole and has lost half its undercarriage, but your kitchen is okay.'

Finally the delivery truck limps into Bir and the gleaming steel pots are unloaded, along with trolleys, huge gas burners and the *momo* oven. The handful of monks left at the institute turn out to watch and cheer. Mal walks through the huge empty room that will house the new kitchen, listening to the head chef explain where he wants it all to go. He has had plenty of time to think about it and has some very definite ideas.

While Mal talks kitchens I finish the final chapter of my book, a month ahead of its deadline. Soon we'll be heading back to Sydney so I can hand it in to the publishers and resign properly from *New Idea*. I'm not looking forward to it. Giving me paid leave was a pretty supportive gesture, and I'm hoping my bosses won't be too annoyed at my decision.

※

Six months is a long time in magazines. I've missed Tom and Nicole's split, Catherine Zeta-Jones and Michael Douglas's wedding, and who knows how many lovers for Fergie and Andrew. I discover also that my boss (the General Manager) and his boss (the Managing Director) have both left the company and I can't find anyone to resign to. There's a new Editor hot to trot in the wings and no-one seems at all fussed that I won't be back. I'm not sure they even remember me. I'm off the hook.

Before we have unpacked, a Sunday gossip column runs a small piece claiming that I'm dating the godson of the Dalai Lama, which comes as news to Mal. A few days later a columnist phones a girlfriend of mine to ask if it's true that I've shaved my head, cut all the legs off my furniture and will only wear orange. She laughs so hard she falls off her chair. When finally she picks herself up and composes herself she thanks him for the best laugh she has had in a long time. She tells him I don't have the cheekbones to go bald, orange makes me look dead and just the night before, she enjoyed way too many wines sitting on my couch and the only things legless were her and me.

After years of being way too interested in other people's private lives, it seems kind of fair that mine should come out looking so bizarre. That would be that karma thing.

2

Two Becomes Three

JUNE 2001

I'm perched on the edge of the bed looking at Mal with a mixture of fear, anticipation and excitement. The little purple ball in a glass vial, the size of my little finger, is doing its thing in the bathroom. It's 1.50 pm. We have ten minutes to see if it turns pink.

It is suddenly quiet in our bedroom overlooking the main street in Bir. The *labrang* we stayed in last year is full so these are our temporary quarters – two rooms on top of the telephone shop run by the deaf-mute Indian man. There is a momentary lull in the endless barrage of noise – no tractor trolleys thundering past on their way to collect the day's pickings from the tea plantations, no barking dogs, and even the rhythmic chanting of hundreds of monks from the surrounding monasteries is momentarily absent. It is as if, like us, everything is temporarily suspended in the sultry heat of a summer afternoon.

I'm aware of the intense worry on Mal's face and my own frantically beating heart. We are a bit stunned at the idea and have just ten minutes to prepare ourselves. We'd talked about this possibility, but only as an abstract concept.

Something's going on. I can feel it in my breasts. They hurt. And I'm out of breath. Just walking up the slight hill to lunch at the Khyentse *labrang* is exhausting. After doing it happily for weeks, now I have to stop for a little rest en route. And I feel kind of hungover, which is really odd because I haven't had a drink since a week ago. That was when we treated ourselves to a weekend at a hotel in Dharamsala – three hours' drive west – and overindulged in room service, beer and TV. Our life in the little monastery village of Bir doesn't feature such luxuries, so to be able to sit up in bed with a curry and a chilled beer watching Robert Redford in *Three Days of the Condor* on cable was our idea of a party.

The colour of that little ball in the glass test tube could mean some major changes. I can't begin to imagine what those changes might be, but there's a gnawing in the pit of my stomach that suggests they will be enormous and ongoing. I keep thinking of that RSPCA advertisement: 'A puppy isn't just for Christmas'. Oh my God, what have we done? It seems a surreal paradox that, while my doctor thinks that at age thirty-nine I'm getting too old to have a baby, I don't actually feel old enough.

In the past twelve months my life has already changed radically. I've swapped my Sydney harbourside apartment, frantic weekly deadlines and regular paypackets to write novels and be with Mal, whose idea of home is wherever he's parked his coffee machine. Its current address is his room in New Delhi in a shared household of westerners and monks, all working for Rinpoche's organisation, Siddhartha's Intent. I've been happily writing wherever Mal's work happens to take us. We've fashioned a wonderfully carefree life together, spending roughly half our time in Sydney and the rest of it hopping on and off planes. I've been able to keep in touch with my agent and publisher via the web, sending chapters and seeing cover designs by email, sometimes crouched in tiny Indian phone booths, other times juggling a laptop and mobile phone in an airport lounge. It's a long way from a slick city office with a personal assistant and all the trappings, but I've been having the time of my life. My first book was well received and I'm well into writing my second, with half-formed ideas for a third, fourth, fifth and so on into old age. The future was looking good for two footloose people with only themselves to worry about, and no responsibilities or commitments. If that little ball turns pink, the changes are unimaginable.

The big hand hits the 12 and our ten minutes are up. We race each other into the bathroom and stare.

It's pink. We're pregnant. Mal is in shock. I'm in shock. We take the little test tube back into the bedroom, carefully lean it against a pile of books and look at it in wonderment for the rest of the afternoon. The next few days we wander around grinning at each other like we have a delicious secret. And I cry, daily.

'Happy tears?' Mal asks anxiously.

'Oh yes,' I say, feeling excited, scared and like an army of hormones is marching through my bloodstream.

We queue at the telephone shop downstairs so that I can ring my best friend in Adelaide and tell her. After writing the phone number down on a piece of paper and passing it to the deaf-mute Indian man, I take my place in the queue of monks.

In the past year the phone man has married, and he signals in sign language across the room to his blushing bride. Like him, she is in her twenties, deaf and mute. She is also breath-takingly beautiful in a red sari with a veil that covers her from head to her tiny bejewelled toes. Their newlywed excitement is palpable and they keep erupting in giggles at some private joke. They make no sound but both their bodies convulse and their faces beam. It is impossible not to join in.

Finally it's my turn, and after shouting my announcement over the dodgy phoneline, all I can do is sob into the receiver.

My friend in Adelaide laughs, the monks laugh and the deaf couple, oblivious to what is going on, are still laughing anyway.

❋

It will be another four months, three continents and vats of hormonal tears before I see the reassuring face of my own doctor in Sydney.

Mal and I find ourselves celebrating the various milestones of pregnancy in a number of different parts of the world. In a hospital in New Delhi I have a series of tests, including an internal ultrasound. Out of respect for my modesty, Mal is not allowed in the room. But every female worker traipses past, interested to know if 'whitey' is the same as them underneath it all. It's like a passing parade by my feet. No-one seems too shocked by what they see, which is something of a relief – although it's a bit hard to tell as no-one gives me eye contact.

I email all the test results to my doctor; he emails back that I'm anaemic and should start iron tablets. I stop sucking in my belly when I'm naked and Mal, with that male candour that is so adorable, expresses surprise that I look pregnant so soon. I tell him that it's a known medical fact that within days of conception a substantial layer of fat is deposited across the mother's belly to keep the embryo warm. Bless him, he believes me.

A few weeks later we're in Paris and go for dinner at the *tres chic* and ultra-cool Buddha Bar. To mark the end of the risk-filled first trimester I lash out and have a sip of red wine then immediately want to throw up.

In London, to visit insurance giant Lloyd's for research on my new book, we have the neuchal translucency ultrasound and the baby waves at us. A heart-stopping moment. In London's Harley Street we meet a colleague of my Sydney doctor, and he explains that the results of the ultrasound are positive. Our odds of producing a Down Syndrome baby given my age just improved from one in thirty-three to one in a hundred. He compares it to the likelihood of being killed on the motorway versus crashing in a plane. It's supposed to be good news but now I'm too scared to get on the next day's flight to America. I spend the trip with my hands wrapped around my belly, just in case.

In New York I have a meeting with a high-powered publisher at St Martin's Press. Standing on Fifth Avenue looking up I realise the office is in the Flat Iron Building, the oldest skyscraper in America and one of the most famous in the world. I'm sure I've seen its distinctive triangular shape in the opening credits for *Friends*. I'm agog. The publisher's office, when I finally find it, is in the pointy end with a view straight up Broadway.

As I take a seat I'm shaking but can't tell whether it is with awe, the effort of not throwing up, or the fact that I desperately need the loo again. It's been twelve minutes since my last visit and I fear the consequences if I don't go again soon.

The publisher tells me she loved my book *Apartment 255*, a dark and twisted thriller set in Sydney, but it disturbed her so much that she couldn't finish it and instead passed it over to three of her editors for appraisal, two of whom are sitting in her office, staring at me suspiciously. 'I was shocked,' says a sweet-looking woman called Hope. 'I was still thinking about it on Tuesday,' adds a man in a suit, leaning away from me as if he fears I may pull out a knife at any moment.

I try to respond but everything is coming to me through a hormonal fog. They are speaking so fast, firing so many questions, that I feel like a rabbit in the headlights, frozen and unable to move (partly because I fear my bladder may leak). I feel limp and exhausted, like I've lost all my stuffing. It's a combination of the heat, my anaemia and the fact that today I'm also making two new little kidneys, or so the pregnancy book says.

I can tell that I'm not what they were expecting – maybe it's the maternity twin-set I bought hurriedly for the occasion – and by the time I leave they no longer look fearful that I am some kind of psycho bunny-boiler. Instead they seem concerned that I won't manage to find my way out of the building.

'Is there someone we can call?' they offer politely. Fortunately Mal is hovering about outside to escort me and my hormones home.

We are staying in New York with some Australian friends who are also expecting a baby, and the wife passes on some useful tips gleaned from a book written in the '50s and given to her by her southern belle secretary. It recommends during pregnancy cutting back martini consumption to just two or three each evening, and to combat morning sickness, it suggests smoking a cigarette before you get out of bed. Just talking about it makes us both race to the bathroom.

Then it is on to Canada where, finally, I blossom. My skin really does glow, just like it says in the book. My energy levels rocket and the nausea passes. It's obvious now that I'm pregnant and people offer all sorts of advice – the only helpful bit being that we should try to get an audience with a renowned female Tibetan lama who lives in Vancouver. She has five children, having popped each one out in just two hours apiece while she continued weaving.

I get very excited and decide that I want to do it that way. I tell Mal I cannot possibly face childbirth without talking to this woman. Through the help of one of her students, who is a friend of Mal's, we are invited for tea.

❋

Jetsun Kushok is a very rare creature – a realised female master of Tibetan Buddhism. She understands the nature of reality in a way that I can't even begin to perceive and has dedicated her life – and the next, and every one after that – to helping the rest of us 'get it'. Her brother is Sakya Trizin, the leader of the Sakya School of Buddhism and in some ways equal in standing to the Dalai Lama. Jetsun is undoubtedly a big kahuna in the Buddhist scheme of things but even more importantly, to my self-centred impure way of thinking, she's someone who might just be able to give me a couple of really helpful pointers, particularly on how to avoid pain. I'm thinking the tantric inner secrets of birth. Woman to woman.

I decide it might be best if Mal doesn't sit in, and try to explain this to him in the car on the way to her home by alluding vaguely to 'secret women's business', raising my eyebrows and nodding a lot. He looks at me with a nervous expression I'm coming to know well: *Is this another hormone moment? What is the safest answer here?*

Jetsun Kushok is a tiny, pragmatic woman who lives without airs and graces in a simple bungalow in suburban Vancouver with her husband, children and grandchildren. She sleeps only a few hours a night and fulfils an exhausting itinerary, criss-crossing the globe to teach her many students.

Perched daintily on the edge of an armchair offering more tea, she could be any suburban grandmother. Almost. There is about her a simplicity and calmness that is hard to identify and impossible to resist. Her face is youthful and her eyes full of compassion. When we tell her I'm pregnant, she looks at me in such an eerie way I feel like she is seeing right into my belly.

'Aaah,' she says with a mysterious smile. And nods. I nod too. I've never been backward in coming forward but find myself completely gobsmacked and cannot think of a thing to say. Mal, thank God he is here, takes over, explaining that we would welcome any advice on pregnancy and childbirth.

She tells me to rub sesame oil on my belly and back twice a week, to walk a lot, and avoid goat and pork. Chicken, beef and lamb are okay. I need to strengthen my kidneys in preparation for the birth. Very important.

During the birth she says to avoid cold or iced drinks but sip tea or water at room temperature or above. Drinking cold things gives the baby a shock, which will cause it to retract and slow things down, she explains, demonstrating by wrapping her arms around herself and shivering.

After the birth she recommends lying in bed on my side to

allow the bones to contract naturally, and to avoid all exercise. In Tibet, women take to their bed for weeks, while their extended family looks after them. She also says to avoid alcohol and eat just smooth soups that won't tax the body in digestion.

Mal is writing down all this wonderful practical advice. Finally, I find the courage to ask the big one. How do I get around the *pain* thing? I understand her births were all quick and relatively painless, and, well, I'd rather like one of those myself . . .

She smiles, her eyes full of wisdom and compassion, then delivers the blow. 'That all depends on your karma,' she says.

Damn. No short cuts here. My karma is undoubtedly light years away from hers. And it's a bit late to try to notch up brownie points now.

I kneel on the carpet for a blessing and she puts her hands on my head and stomach. It is unaccountably moving and warmth spreads through every nerve and muscle. When Mal and I are safely alone in the car again, I burst into tears.

'Happy tears?' he asks, for the umpteenth time.

'Oh yes,' I say, feeling more excited, more scared and like reinforcements have just arrived for that army of hormones still marching through my bloodstream.

⁕

A few months later in Sydney my waters break but it is three days before a drug-induced labour really gets going. When the wall of pain hits, it is so fierce that I take all the drugs on offer. (I decide that at least my karma is good enough that I'm giving birth where such things are available.)

As the sun sets on 11 February 2002, we finally get to meet the most gorgeous little girl in the world. She is sporting a crop of vivid red hair that stands straight up, as if she's just put her finger in an electric socket. She looks up at us with the most enormous and luminous blue eyes. Mal and I both fall hopelessly in love with her.

Very soon we are feeling like the cleverest people in the world. This parenthood thing isn't going to slow us down. *Au contraire.* Having little Miss Kathryn Rose will just make it all the more fun, we tell each other, with all the bravado and naivety of new parents. We buy a high-tech backpack that converts into a pram and when she's just three months old, we get her a passport of her own. She'll be needing it.

We ignore all the tut-tuts and unhelpful advice, and pack her along with our laptops, a suitcase of nappies, a dictionary, thesaurus and a *Spot the Dog* book, and head off to India, where the next stage of Mal's building project is about to begin. That's our life and she just became a most glorious and welcome part of it. We'll just have to figure it out as we go.

3

The Muncles

I pick up an empty plastic bottle of Bisleri water and lick the label. Urrgh. It tastes of dirt and dust. For all I know, this bottle rolled along the streets of Old Delhi on its way here to Bir and is carrying ghastly third-world diseases capable of liquifying all my internal organs, or worse. I lick it again.

I figure there's no time to waste. Whatever germs are on that label I want them in my bloodstream as quickly as possible. I've got to get started on making their antibodies. It's in the book lying by my bedside.

Baby Love by Sydney nurse Robin Barker is a hefty tome and weighs more than all my clothes, but there is no way I was bringing our baffling little five-kilo bundle to one of the most germ-ridden corners of the world without it. On page 64 it says that breastmilk contains antibodies to protect babies from illness. Kathryn, three months old, just licked the label and that's why I'm doing the same, seeking out whatever germs might be lurking there unseen.

During the past few weeks that we've been back in India, Mal and I have been vigilant about what she puts in her mouth, sterilising her four dummies in boiling water every evening and constantly wiping her hands with Dettol wipes. The moment my back is turned, Kathryn picks up the first thing she can reach and licks it.

Maybe my theory works, and I make the necessary antibodies, or maybe it doesn't need to. Whatever the case, she stays healthy. I'm not so lucky.

A few days later I find my gut is twisting and groaning, like I have razorblades slicing through my belly. The bout of dysentery isn't as bad as it could be but the timing couldn't be worse. The loo in our bathroom is blocked and it's a five-minute trek from my bed down a flight of stairs, out into the main street, over the sleeping stray dogs, through the queue of Tibetan monks outside the deaf-mute Indian's telephone shop, to get to a working toilet.

✳

I can't say I wasn't warned. From the moment Kathryn was born, people had been full of advice, mostly horror stories about what happens to babies taken outside the country. We always knew we would be bringing her to India as soon as possible, it just seemed to take everyone else a while to cotton on.

When she was less than twenty-four hours old I sought guidance from the paediatrician who popped his head into my hospital room. 'How old should she be before we take her to India?' I asked.

'Twenty-one.'

'Months?'

'No, years.'

'But her father works there.'

'Then tell him to come home and visit,' he replied.

If I hadn't been still weak from labour I would have decked him.

'It's not that I don't agree with parents taking children travelling,' he added helpfully. 'I took my son to Aspen when he was fourteen. But India has germs. Best you don't go there.'

Time for a new doctor – one who spent less time skiing in Aspen and more time in the real world, or third world, dealing with germs.

It took some searching but I finally found a wonderful kindly paediatrician who had worked in South America. In two hour-long appointments he gave Mal and I a crash course in what to look for, what to do, what to take and when to panic. Confident and happy that we could do this, Mal went on ahead. Kathryn and I would meet up with him in Delhi in five weeks.

After he had gone I did all the paperwork, including signing a statutory declaration at the Indian embassy in Sydney, stating that my baby's father didn't object to me taking her out of the country. I sobbed with Kathryn through all her shots and, most important of all, made sure she didn't forget her father. I printed a life-size photo of Mal's face and glued it to a ruler. Daddy-on-a-stick became Kathryn's constant companion. I also filled a tape with Mal's voice crooning and saved two of his smelly T-shirts for her to wear. Her senses were filled with Daddy – sight, sound and smell. Except for the lack of a body, I doubt she noticed he was gone.

I tried to prepare her for 'change' by putting her to sleep in different rooms of our apartment, moving her pram from the kitchen to the bathroom, wedging it in our miniscule hallway and then outside on the balcony with the birds – Indian mynahs – to serenade her while she slept.

It worked and she made the transition beautifully. From Sydney in winter to India in summer during a heatwave. And she registered no shock that Daddy suddenly had legs. When Mal took her from my arms at Delhi Airport, she snuggled into his neck as if they had never been apart.

We stayed just two days in Delhi before heading to Bir, which was two days too long. I've tried to like the city but

I can't. I hate it. It is the armpit of the earth. And even worse with a baby.

The pollution in summer feels like a dirty, wet towel on the skin. The rancid smell and taste of the air makes me want to vomit. But it is the frustrations of daily life that really would send me insane if I ever had to spend too long here.

Mal has a room in the Siddhartha's Intent offices situated in a nice middle-class enclave in western Delhi. The whole suburb, with thousands of residences and businesses, has been without a working telephone for three months. One night someone dug up all the copper wiring and stole it to resell on the black market. After three agonising months, with letters in the newspapers complaining about businesses going broke, the copper has been replaced but still the telephones don't work. It takes a series of bribes to the linesmen in each area to get the telephones 'reconnected'. At every level of management they are breathtakingly obvious about seeking bribes to do the jobs they are paid to do.

Delhi is so overcrowded and under-resourced that there is not enough electricity to go around. The authorities counter this by cutting the supply to different parts of the city for an indeterminate amount of time – which means at some point during the day the air-conditioning won't work.

With an outside temperature of 47 degrees it didn't take long for the room to heat up and become unbearable, but the real torture was not knowing when it would come back on.

As long as the air-conditioning in Mal's room was running, Kathryn was happy. When it went off we draped her with wet hankies, anxiously trying not to let her overheat but fearful we might overdo it and she would catch a chill. It was a fine balance. One time when it looked like she was becoming distressed, she and I spent the afternoon in the blissfully cool lobby of a five-star hotel, enjoying the passing parade of beautiful rich Indian women, looking glamorous in their saris. I must admit I was rather disappointed when Mal turned up to fetch us. The one advantage of the extreme heat was that it was too hot for mosquitoes.

Nothing in India is simple. The most basic services that I take for granted at home are erratic here and governed by corruption. It seems that no-one in power sticks to the rules or behaves with any degree of morality. I marvel at the good humour of the people who live in the midst of this chaos.

The Siddhartha's Intent house has a huge office on the ground floor and a rabbit warren of bedrooms on the two floors above. People come and go all the time, staying a month or a minute.

There is a washing machine on the roof which everyone shares. It is a feature of summer in Delhi that the heat snap-dries your clothes. By the time you've pegged an item to the line it's dry and you can take it down again. Leave it any longer and it starts to go brown.

⁂

Bir is a complete contrast to Delhi – beautiful, with clean air and friendly, harmonious people. We are renting the same two rooms on the first floor above the telephone shop run by the deaf-mute Indian couple where, exactly one year ago, Kathryn was conceived in a rare moment of privacy. It wasn't quite as hot then and the toilet worked.

The Tibetan man who runs the guesthouse has called in the Indian plumbers to fix ours, and it seems to be taking forever. For the past three days, dozens of them have trooped in and out of our room, staring at me and Kathryn. More Indian men sidle along the window ledge, peering in on their way to inspect the bathroom pipes. Today they remove the whole toilet.

I think the cast of thousands has less to do with the job and more to do with the opportunity of a peek at the white lady and her baby. Every nosy Indian man in Bir must have scored a glimpse by now so I'm hoping the bathroom will

Indian comic strips – I sweep the bedroom floor clean with a soft twig broom. Because of the short handle, there really is only one way to do it and that's squatting. At first it nearly kills me, every muscle screaming out in pain as I maintain the squat and shuffle around the room. I remember with longing how easy it was to keep my Sydney floors clean. Two gay guys used to come in once a week and do them. They did a spot of ironing and other stuff too. Heaven. I wish they were here now. After a few weeks I find the squatting becomes less painful and I reckon I could crack walnuts between these thighs.

Then, housework done, it's time to start the day, so Kathryn and I join Mal across the corridor in our 'office', which has a view over the gold-painted rooftops of a monastery and out to Mal's current project, a new *labrang* for Rinpoche. The old one (where we stayed on my first visit to Bir) is straining at the seams with monks and westerners visiting Bir on Siddhartha's Intent business. The new *labrang*, set behind high bougainvillea-covered walls, will provide more accommodation as well as a series of other buildings, including a chapel and a library.

The office is where Mal and I spend most of our time, working at our laptops while Kathryn plays beside me or sleeps in her rocker. She has discovered her feet and spends many hours happily trying to put them in her mouth. Mal has a desk against the window and a bed beside him to lay out the designs he is working on. I sit on a bed against another wall with my computer on a bamboo bedtray, my dictionary and thesaurus within easy reach. We have two fold-up chairs, a table for the Walkman and its little speakers, and a printer. It's very comfortable, well equipped and because we are at the back of the building, mostly quiet. Being at treetop height, we're often joined by Indian mynahs, which perch on the window ledge to stare at us.

From this elevated position I can see the third-floor windows of a monastery building where I know people are doing three-year retreats. That's three years voluntarily locked away from the world to practise meditation and be alone with their mind. It may also be three years without speaking a word. It sounds terrifying.

Occasionally I glimpse a monk's arm reaching out to tend pigeons that come and go from bird boxes attached to the side of the building. I often wonder what it must be like for the monks in there and how, when the time comes, they will re-emerge into the world. Bir may not be changing as fast as other parts of the globe but still, even modern life on this scale must come as a rude shock.

※

The guesthouse where we are staying is full, the rest of the rooms being rented by visiting monks who are here for a debating competition at Dzongsar Institute. The other monks come down from the institute and all day and late into the evening they work away on old Singer sewing machines, stitching together an enormous marquee. When Kathryn gets a bit bored and wants some action I walk her up the corridor to say hello . . . and to see for myself what's going on. Having a baby is a wonderful foil for nosiness, particularly here where her pale skin and red hair make her such a novelty. Wherever we happen to wander I'm treated to life stories and all the local gossip.

Twice a day Mal, Kathryn and I walk about a kilometre to join Rinpoche's household of monks for meals at the old *labrang*. We use a short cut around the huge stone sheds with galvanised iron roofs that the Indians built for the Tibetans, where they weave rugs on huge looms, hold meetings about community issues and gather on special days for group prayers. Then we cut back onto the road, past homes and up the hill to the old Indian cobbler who sits in the dust outside the gates of Dzongsar Institute. He does a roaring trade repairing monks' shoes. He has work all year, rotating between the four monasteries, staying at each one for a few days then moving on. He must have repaired and re-repaired almost every pair of shoes in Bir. For five rupees (twenty cents) he fixes my sandals.

Unless the weather is really bad the Tibetans hang out on the road outside their homes, gossiping while their children play. What used to take us a few minutes takes ten times as long with Kathryn in a sling on Mal's chest. People come out to see the glow-in-the-dark baby, rushing up with big smiles and greeting her with both hands held palm up, while making a clicking noise with their tongues.

Everyone wants to hold her and every Tibetan baby has to be brought face to face with her. It's fine with us. We think Kathryn is pretty special and here's a whole village of like-minded people lining up to fuss over her.

They say she looks like a porcelain doll, and I guess she does. But they worry I don't dress her warmly enough. India is suffering a heatwave and even though we are in the mountains it is still hot. Some days the temperature skyrockets and we pass out in the middle of the day. Other days it is like Sydney in spring – warm but, unlike Delhi, easily bearable.

Kathryn is wearing an all-in-one cotton babysuit with short sleeves, Mal and I are in T-shirts and so are the Tibetans, but their babies are dressed as if we are on the Tibetan steppes and snow is falling. The women can't understand why we don't dress her better or why she is on Mal's chest not mine. I know what they are thinking: *Poor Mal, that friendly man who designed those nice buildings for Rinpoche. Didn't he get a dud wife?*

We get to the top of the hill and arrive at the *labrang*, discreetly tucked away behind Dzongsar Institute, Rinpoche's monastery. He has another monastery in Bhutan and one at his original seat in Tibet. The Khyentse *labrang*, which Mal designed more than a decade ago, is surrounded by high mud-rendered white walls with vivid pink and red bougainvillea spilling over the top. It is a two-storey, L-shaped brick building that wraps around a courtyard, which is dotted with flowers in old pots and tin cans.

A few monks live here, maintaining it all year round for Rinpoche, and people are always coming and going – Tibetans, Bhutanese, Australians, Americans, English and Canadians. They come to study, practise meditation or because they are working on one of the dizzying number of projects Rinpoche has on the go.

The most extraordinary and ambitious project is his Peace Vase Program, which aims to place 6200 vases at strategic points around the world to restore peace, harmony and well-being. Each vase is a sacred container filled with medicines and precious substances. Rinpoche inherited the project from Dilgo Khyentse Rinpoche, one of the greatest Tibetan teachers of the twentieth century. Since 1991 more than 4000 vases have been buried in places as far apart as Antarctica, the remote mountains of northern Iraq, the Great Barrier Reef in Australia, Washington DC, the Colorado Desert, the Amazon rainforest, Jerusalem and the Caribbean. There are around 2000 vases, which Dilgo Khyentse Rinpoche consecrated before he died, still in India ready for placement. They are earmarked for parts of the Middle East, Croatia, Russia and some war-torn African countries. Eventually vases will rest in places of spiritual significance to the native people of every country, in places of war or strife, and in ecologically degraded or endangered natural sites, as well as being buried in every country's capital city, largest mountain range and river system.

The vases are carried to some of the more remote locations by all sorts of people, some not connected to Rinpoche, but who hear about the project and volunteer to take a vase along with them.

Rinpoche also heads Khyentse Foundation, an international organisation that raises money to fund his monasteries and the restoration of rare Buddhist texts in danger of being lost with the destruction of thousands of libraries in Tibet. And here in Bir another of Rinpoche's organisations, Lotus Outreach, provides education, sponsorship and training to children of Tibetan refugees. It also operates in urban Indian slums, bringing education and a new way of life to the children.

Then of course there are his retreat centres in Canada, Bhutan and Australia; his teaching schedule that keeps him criss-crossing the globe constantly; and his films. With so much going on and so many different people passing through, the conversation around the *labrang* table is always interesting.

Lunch is laid out buffet style – rice, *dhal*, chillies and a couple of vegetable dishes, occasionally some boiled meat – and it's always a jolly affair. Mal has known these monks for years and shares their passion for soccer. The World Cup is currently playing and if a match is on during mealtime, it becomes like a scene from *The Cup*, with table thumping, groaning and yelling as each goal is fought. If it's between two hot contenders, the room can be crowded with extra monks from the institute ducking classes to watch.

If there isn't a game on, there's always *The Khyentse News* to catch up on. Valerie Kennedy, a teacher from Byron Bay and long-time student of Rinpoche's, is living here for a few months studying and practising meditation, as well as teaching English to some of the household monks and others from the institute. As part of Valerie's classes, the monks handwrite in English a newspaper reporting on the goings-on in the household over the past twenty-four hours. It is hilarious as well as informative, often explaining for us who the new faces are around the table.

The monks mostly come from huge extended families and they all love a baby. Kathryn is passed backwards and forwards across the table like a salt shaker. Each monk coos and makes faces, anything to get a smile. Two monks in particular have an amazing rapport with her.

Ugyen Thrinley is a relative newcomer at Bir. He had a career in the public service of Bhutan but a few years ago decided he wanted to take robes, so he sought out Rinpoche and volunteered. He is in his early thirties with bulging biceps and, while I'm sure I'm not supposed to notice, is utterly gorgeous. He oversees the building projects when Mal is away and keeps in touch by telephone and email.

Jamyang Zangpo is in his mid forties and walked here from Dzongsar in Tibet in the early '90s. He arrived at the institute and the principal suggested he take robes. Despite having a wife and child back in Tibet, he agreed, and has been here ever since. He has the kindest face, with crinkly eyes that make it look like he's laughing even when he's not.

The two of them are thoroughly besotted with Kathryn. Sometimes they come down to our office to go through building accounts with Mal, but if Kathryn is in the room and awake, Mal can forget about doing business. Some meetings happen with her asleep on Ugyen Thrinley's knee. Mal has dubbed them the 'Muncles'.

The rest of the household is made up of a younger monk, Jampal, and Sonam Choepel, who has a wicked sense of humour. Known as the joker, he was brought up with Rinpoche. Their fathers fled Tibet together, settling in Bhutan, and they were two naughty little boys, constantly getting up to mischief. When Rinpoche was recognised at age seven as a *tulku* (a reincarnate lama), he was taken away to Sikkim to be raised in a monastery and they didn't see each other for many years.

During the next seven years Rinpoche lived a secluded life having private tuition in the Sikkimese King's palace chapel at Gangtok, at one stage not going outside for two years. Meanwhile Sonam Choepel stayed in east Bhutan, became a monk and studied traditional arts. As an adult, Rinpoche sought out his old childhood friend and invited him to become a senior attendant.

In the 1980s Sonam Choepel asked Rinpoche for a few weeks' leave to go home to Bhutan to see his family. Rinpoche didn't see him again for nine years. Sonam Choepel gave no explanation for where he had been or what he had been doing, reappearing one day as if that was perfectly normal. When pressed for an explanation he handed Rinpoche three beautifully decorated wooden masks and said he had been making them for him. That's all he's ever said on the subject. There are rumours of a wife and a child but no evidence either way. He doesn't confirm or deny anything, just gives a cheeky grin.

He's also incredibly kind. When Mal and Kathryn appeared without me for lunch one day – while I was suffering the effects of the Bisleri bottle and didn't have the energy to walk up the hill – he sent back messages of concern and a heatproof container filled with rice, *dhal* and vegetables.

The household is trying out a new cook. Rooplal is a young Nepalese man who dresses like he just stepped from a Calvin Klein catalogue. His outfit looks strangely out of place in this setting. It's hot and the monks are wearing just the bottom halves of their robes and singlets, while we westerners are beyond casual in sweaty T-shirts and sandals. But Rooplal is resplendent in polo-neck sweater, navy blazer and leather slip-ons. He is as fastidious about his kitchen as he is about his dress. Everything is clean and orderly. He hovers anxiously as we help ourselves to the food – nothing Nepalese or Indian, but Bhutanese-style fried vegetables, rice and the ever-present chillies.

He has a wife and family back in Nepal and, at A$150 a month, this is a good job. He looks pleased when everyone at the table agrees that the food is sensational, even better than the previous cook, who was a monk and highly popular. To be rated better than him is big indeed.

Rooplal saves all the kitchen scraps for the *labrang* dog, an Alsatian called Simba. She and her puppies live in a kennel in the courtyard under a huge weeping willow. Also in the court-yard is a small glass-walled lamphouse with hundreds of butter lamps, which are constantly burning. The lamphouse is tended by Tsering Wangpo, a stooped man with a heavily lined face who must be in his eighties or nineties. He keeps to himself, taking his meals alone. He was a Tibetan freedom fighter, and killed his fair share of Chinese soldiers. When the Dalai Lama asked the fighters to put down their weapons, telling them that the Tibetan way was peace, Tsering Wangpo was so filled with remorse he found his way to Bir and dedicated the rest of his life to making offerings to Buddha. He rises every morning at 3 o'clock to tend the butter lamps and sweep out the lamp-house.

He also sweeps the courtyard and the walkway outside the front gate. He is so diligent and thorough that not a blade of grass or seed escapes his broom, which leaves just huge patches of dry dirt or, when it rains, mud. The monks would be happy to let some grass grow, but they are even happier to let Tsering Wangpo do his thing and wouldn't dream of interfering.

※

One day on our way home after lunch we stop at the huge wrought-iron entry gates of Dzongsar Institute. Inside, hundreds of monks are seated under the enormous marquee, beautifully decorated with hand-painted dragons and auspicious symbols. The monks are doing prayers together before tonight's debating competition. It's an awesome sight.

Seated in two huge blocks facing each other, they wave their hands in unison as they perform elegant *mudra*s (kind of a hand ballet) and chant. It is a wonderfully deep, rich sound that swells and rises, bouncing off the walls of the institute and resonating around the huge quadrangle. Kathryn, awake and alert in the sling on Mal's chest, starts waving her arms and legs with excitement.

Mal leads us through the gate to a spot where we can watch what's going on. Five hundred pairs of eyes swing around to look at us. The faces break into huge grins. Mal and I never caused this sort of reaction on our own. It's that glow-in-the-dark baby again.

We watch mesmerised for a few minutes then a mighty ear-splitting burst of thunder heralds that a storm is imminent. It is a feature of the topography and proximity to the mountains that as monsoon season approaches, every few days we are treated to massive, sudden storms. They are awe-inspiring.

Dark clouds gather at the top of the mountains and either blow off in another direction or sweep on down the valley, bringing a wild angry electrical storm. Then it passes and the sky clears ready for another fabulous sunset.

※

There is only one drawback to life in Bir – the telephones. The lines, when they are working, are fine for a chat but not good enough for the transmission of data, which means we can't send or receive emails. To do that we have to go to the nearby town of Chauntra. It's only four kilometres away but, like everywhere in India, the roads are so bad it takes about twenty minutes by rickshaw or taxi.

It's not much fun for Kathryn – bouncing in and out of potholes the size of small swimming pools – so every few days Mal takes both our computers and disappears for a few hours. And thank God he does. Otherwise we wouldn't realise how close we are to certain death – by nuclear bomb, launched by Pakistan. Due any minute.

It takes hysterical emails from Australia to alert us to this fact.

'Alexander Downer said on tonight's news that you have to come home now or he won't be responsible for you!' says one, making us wonder if the Foreign Minister had indeed gone on national television to personally warn Bunty, Mal and Kathryn.

'We hear that there is a mass exodus out of India and no-one can get flights. How awful for you to be so trapped,' said another.

Trapped? Is she joking? I never want to leave this idyll.

The Indian Express, our only window to the world outside Bir, has been keeping us up to date on the rising tensions in Kashmir, 100 kilometres up the road from here. But they reflect nothing of the hysteria that appears to have gripped the Australian newspapers. I gather they are running maps showing how much of the fallout from a nuclear bomb will reach different parts of Australia. My girlfriend in Adelaide sends me emails saying that she is beside herself with worry. We try to reconcile that image with what we are seeing around us.

When we came to Bir two weeks ago we caught the overnight train from Delhi to Pathankot, the train station near the border of Pakistan. Soldiers are always milling about there on their way to and from the military camps. This trip through Pathankot was no different and security was about as lax as always. As we drove past the officers' camp they were spending the morning enjoying a leisurely game of golf. If war was about to break out, they seemed remarkably sanguine. And the closer we got to the supposed 'front', the more peaceful it seemed to be.

As for the people in Bir, they are delightfully unfussed. The biggest deal here is whether the electricity will hold out long enough to see the next World Cup match, when the monsoons will arrive, and how cheap the mangoes are as India is enjoying an unexpected glut. We may be close to Kashmir and Pakistan geographically, but we're a thousand miles away in every other possible way.

I decide that if the fallout maps are right and Australia would be so badly affected by a nuclear bomb detonated here, then what the hell. Why go home? We may as well stay here and enjoy the mangoes. I maintain this nonchalant attitude until a western doctor friend studying in Dharamsala comes for a visit one pleasant Tuesday afternoon.

She tells us, over tea and biscuits in our office, that the war will start on Thursday. The way she says it, with such certainty, makes it sound like India and Pakistan have made a booking. Some friends in Dharamsala told her, she says. They have friends in the Pakistani military. It seems surreal, but she is adamant. First thing Thursday morning a cell from the Pakistan army will crawl over the border, deliberately provoking the Indian military into unleashing its nuclear bomb on Pakistan, who will send one straight back into India. It's too late for us to leave. We're all going to die. She smiles and takes another biscuit.

After she leaves I express some misgivings to Mal, who rolls his eyes.

'How is it that a western doctor knows the top-secret plans of the Pakistani military?' he asks.

Mmm.

Thursday comes and goes and there is no tell-tale mushroom cloud over the monastery roofs to the west. It's the same serene blue, going on forever. But I think I won't really believe it until I read Friday's newspaper, reporting on Thursday's news, which we will get on Saturday. I scan it anxiously over my morning cup of tea. Not a mention. No-one nuked us on Thursday. I breathe a huge sigh of relief.

Being here in Bir we see the different international reactions. The west claims the threat of war is very real and start pulling out non-essential staff from embassies and closing some of the international schools. The Indians are furious, saying it is an overreaction and undiplomatic. One Indian Government minister is highly indignant, claiming western minds just don't understand the reality of the situation.

'Don't they realise it's just bluster?' he is quoted as saying.

Thank you for the clarification.

※

Meanwhile, for us, life goes on. A pair of Indian salesmen drive half a day from Chandigargh to come and talk solar panels with Mal. He wants to install them on the roof of Dzongsar Institute to power the hot water used in the new kitchen.

They come for a meeting in our office. I hear them arrive and see across the door how formally they behave with Mal, bowing a lot, shaking his hand and handing him business cards. They are so businesslike and professional in their suits, despite the heat. Mal hasn't shaved, but at least his T-shirt is clean. I take them tea and, in recognition of the important meeting, keep my head demurely bowed, just like a good Indian wife.

They ask for sugar. Of course. Indians love their tea sweet – so achingly sweet it gives me lockjaw. Neither Mal nor I take sugar so I apologise profusely and race out to buy some, tucking Kathryn into her rocker beside them before I disappear down the hallway. There is a little Tibetan grocery shop a few doors up. The man pours a small pile of sugar – probably a couple of dessertspoons – from a large container onto a newspaper, then deftly wraps it. He waves away my money. We are regulars here, buying cold drinks and water each day, and he thinks this amount is too small to mention. He's a good businessman. Competition must be keen as the shops on either side of him look identical and sell the same products.

India's emerging consumer class is a huge untapped market and is starting to be bombarded with products by all the multinational grocery companies. Most of the big-name brands available in Sydney can be found on the shelves of these small shops that are the size and shape of a single car garage. Fizzy drinks, shampoo and conditioner, baby formula, tinned sardines and tuna, washing powder, even jars of olives.

I rejoin the men for their meeting, placing the sugar in a little jar in front of them. They use it all.

Often I've gone along with Mal to source different building products and the Indian men have ignored me, refusing to make eye contact with me or even acknowledge I'm in the room. Such is the status of women. But these men, two brothers, are utterly charming. And they know their solar panels. They produce a photo album of successful projects they have completed, proudly showing us their *pièce de résistance*, the solar heating they installed for a swimming pool at an exclusive Indian girls school.

They make the best 'collectors' in India, they say. That's the black box that traps the sun's heat, possibly the most crucial component of a good solar system. They are so passionate about their business that I can't help but be enthralled. By the end of the meeting I'm agreeing that certain types of hoses are indeed 'elegant' and theirs are undoubtedly the best-looking 'widgets' I've ever seen.

The brothers and their handsome widgets live in a little factory on an industrial estate in the city of Chandigargh, 240 kilometres north of Delhi, where Mal and I stayed once when instead of catching the train from Delhi, we decided to drive overland to Bir. Chandigargh, designed in the 1950s by French architect and town planner Le Corbusier, is home to one of the wonders of the modern world, and I am excited to discover that these men are from that extraordinary city. They are equally as delighted to meet a fan.

In the midst of the vast barren dust bowl that is India, Chandigargh contains a public park that almost defies belief. It is a garbage dump that has been turned into a surreal sculptural garden.

While the new city was being built, amid much fanfare and excitement, a roads inspector quietly and systematically collected all the building refuse – broken tiles and glass, ceramic toilet bowls, bottles, rags, electrical fixtures, bits of crockery, car parts, plastic bangles and terracotta pots. On the back of his bicycle he carried what he had found and hid it in a disused wasteland on the outskirts of town. Unauthorised development of any kind was strictly illegal in the fancy new city, so secretly each night, by the light of burning tyres, he worked, recycling the garbage. He turned it into exotic creative sculptures.

In 1972 a government party stumbled across the illegal development hidden in the forest. By then it was a fantasy garden of twenty-three acres or more, featuring almost 2000 sculptures ranging from small to life size and bigger – animals, people and deities, entire miniature villages, all set into the natural rocky labyrinth of the wasteland.

Word spread and soon people were visiting from all over India and the world. Nek Chand, the uneducated and unas-suming roads inspector, became a world-celebrated artist. He has had exhibitions in Paris, London, Berlin and Madrid, and donated over a hundred sculptures to the Capital Children's Museum in Washington. He spent six months installing them and running workshops, sharing his vision for urban recycling. Nek Chand still lives at the site and is working on completing new, ever more ambitious sculptures.

The day we visited, in March 2001, was so hot it felt like there wasn't enough air to breathe, but we persevered, inspecting every inch of the fantasy world he had created from garbage. It seems to encapsulate my experience of India. Just when I am convinced I hate it and can stand no more poverty, dirt or sleazy advances, something wonderfully magic and unexpected will just bowl me over.

※

It's payday at the new *labrang* worksite and Mal strolls around with Kathryn on his chest and an umbrella over them both while I walk behind handing out sweets. I feel like a complete ponce, recreating some old black-and-white movie of the days of the Raj.

The Indian workers crowd around to touch Kathryn and congratulate Mal. This group of a dozen or so women have worked on various projects for him over the past ten years, and their obvious delight at meeting his baby is lovely. There are lots of smiles and hands held in prayer, touching their forehead in blessing to us both.

The women, the same ones we hear walking down the main street at 7 am on their way to the site, are covered neck to foot in beautiful vivid saris. They toss the *dupatta* (shawl) over their shoulder and out of their way to get down to work. And backbreaking work it is. Some carry piles of gravel on trays on their heads. Others work in pairs, one wielding a shovel of gravel and the other helping take its weight by an attached rope. They bring their lunch in *tiffin* boxes, small stainless-steel food containers stacked on top of each other.

They work seven days a week and the end of each month is payday, when they finish early, cook a chicken or two and Mal provides alcohol for a party. They are paid about A$2.50 a day, which is the upper level for unskilled labour. Most of the women are married and their husbands work on their farms, or as skilled workers elsewhere.

The most exciting day is when they pour the concrete, and Kathryn and I wander down to watch all the fun. After weeks of preparation (formwork, placing steel and laying plastic conduit for electrical cables), workers come from all over the valley to help. It is a bit like the scene in *Witness* when all the Amish men work together to build a barn. There is a real sense of camaraderie and co-operation here, as well as urgency. Once water is added to the cement powder, sand and gravel, and ground through the hand mixer, it doesn't take long to set, particularly in this warm, dry weather.

The Indians – men of all ages, dressed in shorts, some with impossibly skinny, bowed legs – twist their scarves into a cushion on their head and form a queue. They wait patiently, jostling each other and grinning. As soon as the first batch of concrete is ready they are off, holding out big tin cans or metal trays for the cement mixer to pile on sloppy, wet concrete. They hoist these onto their heads and, balancing them with one hand, make their way quickly and expertly up a series of bamboo ladders, along exposed beams to where it is needed. They dump it for the women to smooth into place, and file back, passing each other on the ladders. There must be fifty or sixty of them, pouring a few cubic metres of concrete.

The women bring thermoses of sweet *chai* (tea) and share them out during a break, offering cups to Kathryn and me. At the end of the day, everyone is exhausted but the sense of satisfaction is contagious. What started out as a skeleton is beginning to look like the three-storey accommodation building that it will eventually become.

※

While building progresses around her, and I finish off my book, Kathryn has been achieving her own significant milestones. She has discovered she can fit both feet into her mouth, hold her head up on her own and vocalise a string of sounds that could be anything. Possibly Swahili, maybe Tibetan – though the monks have no more idea what she is saying than we do, which makes that unlikely. It's just baby babble, but all the same, we are ridiculously proud.

Our time in Bir is up and we take her back to Sydney – happy to show off all her new tricks.

4

Men of Magic

SEPTEMBER 2002

Would Kathryn and I like to spend three months in Bhutan sleeping on the floor with twenty strangers whose names I can't pronounce, while he disappears up a yak trail six hours away, not even accessible by carrier pigeon?

Of course, Mal doesn't put it quite like that. Not at first. He says Rinpoche is making a new movie, bigger and more sophisticated than *The Cup* and this time set in Bhutan. Mal and Raymond Steiner are again co-producers, which means Mal will have to spend three months there. He thinks he might be able to organise for Kathryn and I to stay with a lovely local family throughout the shoot. What do I think?

Over a glass of chilled chardonnay on a balmy night in Sydney, with Kathryn clean, fed and asleep in her cot, it sounds impossibly exotic. We three survived India in a heatwave. Compared to that, surely, Bhutan will be a breeze.

Mal adds a few more touches. While he works and lives in makeshift camps, knee deep in mud and filmset dramas,

Kathryn and I would be comfortably ensconced with this family of six sisters, two of whom have married brothers, and all their extended offspring. There'll be children for Kathryn to play with, people to help me look after her while I write, and Mal would visit every few days. All of this in one of the most mysterious countries of the world, Bhutan. Land of the Thunder Dragon.

I know little of the country and yet something is ringing a faint bell. Wasn't it the fabled Shangri-la of James Hilton's 1933 novel *Lost Horizon*? For some unknown reason my sixth-grade teacher gave that to me to read when I was just twelve years old. I'd been enthralled by the mysticism and magic. We could go *there* for three months? To that secretive little kingdom, bordered by India and Tibet, nestled among the clouds on the roof of the world, where time has stood still . . . when do we leave? I'm beside myself with excitement at the adventure of it all.

Friends say how *brave* they think I am, in a tone that reveals they think no such thing. Clearly I'm suffering some sort of postnatal lunacy. One woman in my new mothercare group is outraged on Kathryn's behalf. Fancy taking a little baby to one of the coldest regions of the world and, worse still, away from western medicine. What if . . . ? Yes, indeed. What if all sorts of things happen, none of them good? Like, I'm not already waking in the middle of the night drenched in sweat at all the possibilities. But I figure this is part of the parenthood deal and while I know I'm new at it, I think it has little to do with geography.

Our Kathryn is fit and healthy, with the sweetest disposition you could hope for, and, at just three months, she survived the rough and tumble of travelling in India. She is *sooo* much bigger now – seven months and thriving. I think it's better for us to be together with her dad, under any conditions, than away from him. Travelling is part of Mal's job and how we live our life. Spending three months in Bhutan sounds like a glorious opportunity. I think I would be crazy to say no.

So it's settled. We are going. Mal flies on ahead and we prepare to follow him in five weeks. Daddy-on-a-stick comes out of the drawer, Kathryn has more shots and I start searching for thermal babywear in Sydney in spring.

※

I don't even make it onto the plane before Kathryn and I get into trouble, trapped in the huge revolving doors of Sydney Airport. It is a pivotal moment as, with a crashing thud, I realise that my old solo life has gone forever. Jetting around the world with a baby on my hip was never meant to be like this.

I stand mute and helpless, Kathryn crying loudly, while I try to juggle her in her state-of-the-art travelling pram along with a trolley carrying a travel cot, the biggest suitcase I have ever owned (full of nappies, baby food, a Bamix and her thermal clothing), as well as an outrageous amount of hand luggage – a laptop computer plus her supplies for the next thirty-six hours. Inside the revolving doors all noise is muffled. It's like being in a huge fish bowl. Everyone can see me but no-one comes to help. I feel waves of disapproval. *Babies aren't welcome here. It's an airport, don't you know?*

I don't have enough hands to push a trolley and a pram, and we become wedged in the airlock. It takes every ounce of strength but eventually I push the trolley so hard against the bulletproof/childproof/terroristproof glass door that it budges, millimetre by millimetre, until finally we stumble out to join the airport chaos.

※

Getting into Bhutan is hard work for anyone. You can't just buy an air ticket at your local travel agency and fly on in. Bhutan's only airline, Druk Air, won't issue a ticket to a foreigner without a visa from the Foreign Ministry in Thimphu. And the only place to collect that is inside the country, at Bhutan's international airport in Paro.

It's complicated, confusing and usually handled by travel operators (for an organised tour) or diplomatic channels (for people coming in on business).

Kathryn and I fall outside either of these categories, which makes it a bit harder. Mal has left me with a file of documents, including a letter from his Bhutanese friends, Mani Dorji and Karma Yangki, confirming that we are their invited guests. I read it standing in the queue at the Druk Air counter at Bangkok airport at 4 am and wish I had paid more attention to how Mal pronounced the names.

The Druk Air people are pleased to see Kathryn but shake their head over our mountain of luggage. It's a small plane with strict weight quotas so they charge an extra A$330, a staggering amount just to get Kathryn's luggage to Bhutan – she only weighs six kilos. The pre-dawn check-in is because of the fierce winds that sweep across Paro Valley each afternoon. They make landing difficult, so all planes must be safely on the tarmac before noon.

The flight itself is one of the most awesome in the world, with the plane following the face of the Himalayas. Mal has briefed me well: the best place to view it is at the back, on the left. By the time I get Kathryn, all our luggage and paperwork to the correct counter, we are allocated the last remaining seat – the front right-hand side, wedged into the curve of the plane, my knees, nose and baby pressed hard against the wall dividing us from the half-dozen business class passengers.

Fortunately, Kathryn just sleeps. It has something to do with the vibration of the engines. As soon as we take off, her little head bobs a few times and she's out. I give up any idea of struggling past everybody for a visit to the loo, or even crossing my legs, and settle in to think about something else for the five-hour flight.

We stop briefly in India at Kolkata (formerly Calcutta) to pick up more passengers. The plane is now crammed full, every one of the seventy-two seats taken. Next to me is a large Indian woman, who lets me know straight away she doesn't like babies. And I didn't even have to ask.

We reach altitude and the pilot announces that there's a problem with an engine and we'll be returning to Kolkata Airport. A ripple of fear runs up and down the aisle which I manage to keep in check until the flight attendant – amazingly handsome, like a young Elvis Presley but with more feline eyes – leans across my Indian friend and her husband to whisper so that only I can hear: 'Make sure you hold on tightly to your baby. The landing could be . . . difficult.'

Now I do want to panic – if only I had the room.

Indeed it is a rocky landing, causing Kathryn to vomit all over my white long-sleeved cotton shirt. We taxi across the tarmac, stopping well short of the terminal, and are told to leave our personal belongings, take just our passports, and get off the plane. No-one needs to be told twice. All the passengers are off in a heartbeat, the woman with the baby naturally being left till last.

I've noticed that on a plane, having a baby makes me less than popular. In an emergency, I'm beyond the status of leper.

I have plenty of time to calmly collect some nappies and baby food, coo with Kathryn (who, having vomited up the contents of her stomach, now is blissfully unfussed), and then chase after the fleeing mob.

Inside Kolkata terminal we are kept in a large hot room. As the sun rises higher in the sky, everything starts to smell – the room, the tarmac – but most of all Kathryn and me. We are putrid. A fresh nappy fixes her and I try to rinse her vomit off me with cold water, but it doesn't stop the bitter tang of her gastric juices from following me like a cloud. Just the smell of vomit makes me want to vomit. I try to breathe as shallowly as possible and, as there is a hot breeze blowing through the open doors, keep downwind of the other passengers. After a few sweaty hungry hours we are told everything is okay, the problem has been fixed and we can board again.

The elderly couple behind me (on a package tour from Alaska) spend much of the takeoff loudly discussing where the smell of vomit is coming from. The flight takes an hour and I hear lots of oohs and aaahs from the back on the other side of the plane as Mount Everest is spotted, soaring above the row of jagged peaks that poke through the sky. I try to join in the excitement and press my head hard against the seat on a sharp right angle so that I can just make out a triangle of vivid blue above the wing.

That decision proves to be a mistake. Flying into Paro is quite simply *terrifying*. Even worse than navigating the high-rise buildings on the approach to the old Hong Kong airport.

The plane flies frighteningly close to the mountains, heads straight for one particular peak, does a sudden last-minute turn, then drops out of the sky, soaring so low over fields and farm roofs that I am sure I could reach out and touch them. We land just centimetres from the end of the runway. Paro Airport has one of the shortest runways in the world – just 1830 metres – and the planes need every precious millimetre of it to pull up in time.

All in all it is undoubtedly the worst and most uncomfortable trip of my life, which is a surprise to Mal, who greets me with a hearty 'Isn't the flight fabulous?' It could be worse. He could tell me I stink. As it is, he doesn't notice. He hasn't showered for days and smells about as good as I do.

For the past few weeks he's been staying at an old logging camp, nearly 4000 metres above sea level at a place called Chelela. It's primitive and cold. 'Showering' is done standing naked with a bucket of hot water and a plastic jug to pour it over you. Under those conditions Mal decided washing just wasn't a high priority. Bed has been a mattress on the floor in a draughty wooden hut. While the cast and camera crew have been a few kilometres up the road shooting, Mal has spent most of his time on that bed, running the production from his laptop computer, with a walkie-talkie to talk to people on the set and a Bhutanese remote telephone to keep in touch with the world.

Mobile networks aren't up and running in the country yet but Mal has bought long-distance remote phones. As long as he stays within a few kilometres of the base station, kept in a local man's bedroom, he can talk to anyone, though the cost is astronomically high.

Kathryn and I arrive a few weeks into filming, just as they have finished on the first location – a small wooden hut deep in the forest – and are moving to the next, the luxurious Kichu resort in Paro. When Mal picks us up from the airport he takes us straight there.

*

There are sixteen foreigners working on the film, including Hollywood lighting designer Ray Peschke, who turned down a couple of huge Hollywood movies to be here, and cinematographer Alan Kozlowski, whose special effects company won Oscars for *Independence Day* and the Robin Williams film *What Dreams May Come*. This film, *Travellers & Magicians*, tells the story of a young man who wants to leave behind old Bhutan with its quaint ways and simple joys to find a glamourous new life in America. He shares his journey across Bhutan with a group of travellers, including a monk, who annoys him with irritating truths hidden in a mystical story he weaves along the way, a story of magic, seduction, desire and murder. It is a story within a story.

Part of Rinpoche's vision in bringing film-making foreigners into the country is that the fledgling local video industry should benefit. Each foreigner has been teamed with a Bhutanese assistant, eager to learn more about the film business but even more eager to work for Rinpoche, who in this part of the globe is bigger than anyone Hollywood could ever produce.

In Bhutan, Tibet and the Buddhist world, Rinpoche is His Eminence Dzongsar Jamyang Khyentse Rinpoche, revered as a meditation master, a reincarnate lama, who was removed from his family and raised by monks. Throughout his childhood he received instruction from the greatest Tibetan masters of this era. He is the reincarnation and lineage holder of the great nineteenth-century master Jamyang Khyentse Wangpo. In terms of Vajrayana Buddhism (also called Tibetan Buddhism or Himalayan Buddhism), they don't come much bigger. To the film world he is known simply as Khyentse Norbu, the movie-making lama.

Some of the foreigners are Rinpoche's students and, like Mal, worked with him on his first movie. They have some idea of his maverick style. The newcomers – cinema heavyweights from Hollywood and Australia – have no idea what they have let themselves in for.

The date for the first day of shooting, 29 September 2002, was set by *mo*, which is a form of divination done by beads or dice. In this case it was performed by another high Tibetan lama, Orgyen Tobgyal Rinpoche, who specialises in such things. He performed *mo*s for many production decisions on *The Cup*, including hiring the crew. One *mo* concerned hiring award-winning film editors John Scott and Lisa-Anne Morris, who were in Paris when they received a call from their agent telling them they had been 'chosen' to work on a film with a first-time writer and director, someone they had never heard of, called Rinpoche. With no understanding of anything Buddhist, it is a testament to their sense of adventure that they said yes. The way John tells it, someone ringing out of the blue to say he'd been 'chosen' by the universe to work on a project was a pretty compelling invitation. He couldn't imagine how he could have said no.

Mal was used to working this way but it must have seemed like bizarre behaviour to some of the foreign crew.

For the two weeks leading up to the nominated first day of shooting, it rained heavily. Buckets and buckets of it poured down. Their living quarters were awash with mud, lighting equipment was delayed en route from India, and everybody was miserable.

But, right on cue, the morning of 29 September dawned bright and crisp, not a cloud in the azure sky.

Before a single frame could be shot, Rinpoche conducted a *puja*, a ceremony to make offerings to the local deities, and invited everyone working on the film to participate. Possibly it was at this moment, breathing in clouds of pungent smoke and watching maroon-robed monks pour bottles of whisky into a fire, that the new crew got the hint: this was not going to be an ordinary shoot.

※

Mal fills me in on it all as we drive through Paro Valley. It is strikingly beautiful, with willow trees lining the roads and terraced rice paddies rising up slowly to the craggy Black Mountain range. The soil is fertile and agriculture thrives, making this one of the wealthier regions.

It also features some of the oldest and most spectacular buildings, specifically the Bhutanese *dzong*s, immense white fortresses built on hilltops and ridges throughout the country. Usually they are made up of two wings that house the government and monastery offices, with a courtyard in between. They are often so enormous that entire villages could find refuge there during wars. Each *dzong* is made up of a series of buildings with cantilevered roofs that follow the contour of the ridge or hill. The walls are inward sloping, which has the effect of making them appear even larger. Amazingly, they were built without blueprints or a single nail.

One of the country's most impressive *dzong*s is in Paro. It is an extraordinary sight, dominating the landscape. Bernardo Bertolucci chose it for some of his 1993 film *Little Buddha*, on which Rinpoche worked as a consultant. While Rinpoche was the expert on all things Buddhist, he took the opportunity to learn cinema techniques from the great film-making master Bertolucci.

I start to get a sense of how differently they do things here when we drive down the main street of Paro. Some of the shops have a ladder through their front window – that's how you get in.

Kathryn and I are very happy to be reunited with Mal. For the next forty-eight hours she won't let him go, or he won't let her go. I'm not sure which. She spends every moment – awake or asleep – snuggled into his chest in a baby sling.

❋

Filming is going well and the cast and crew make us welcome, but it is a busy schedule so we really only see them at meals, which are rowdy buffet affairs held at a long table in the resort dining hall. The food is great but not so appealing to a baby just getting used to solids. If you take out the curries, the pig fat and the really odorous cheese, it doesn't leave much. I carefully hide my solitary jar of Vegemite in her pram when we come to breakfast. It's one thing I know she will eat but, with half-a-dozen Australians in the crew, there's not enough to share it around. I feel like an idiot when I see similar jars dotted along the table and realise every Aussie has brought their own.

After weeks in camp, the crew's conversation centres mostly around the hot shower they just had and their comfortable beds, or they dissect the day's shooting. For Kathryn and I the days are long and lazy, mostly spent hanging out in the resort. I write when she sleeps and take her for long walks among the wildflowers by the river when she is awake.

For everybody else, it's stress city. In many ways this film is a pressure cooker. The foreign crew members are mostly strangers, from all over the world – Australia, Canada, Germany and America. They are getting to know each other as they work, adapting to the high altitude and fiercely cold environment, all while living rough. That's on the personal side. On the professional side they are shooting a film in a language they don't understand, working to a tight budget and schedule, with no margin for delays.

They are all creative people, and Rinpoche welcomes everyone's input. That sounds simple enough but is not usually the way film-making works, where everyone has clearly defined roles. On the set of this film, it takes some a bit longer than others to get used to. The first weeks were fraught with creative differences and clashes of egos – among the westerners, that is.

Normally crews spend weeks in pre-production meetings in which every department (make-up, wardrobe, grips, lighting, camera, sound) goes through each scene to work out what will be required of them. Because the crew live in different countries and the film budget didn't allow for getting them together before filming, pre-production was done mostly through emails, telephone calls and a website where everything available was posted, from photos of the cast and locations, to maps. The idea was for everybody to log in and get some sense of the place. But because Bhutan is such an extraordinary country, with its own way of doing things, none of them really knew what to expect.

So the first weeks were tough as they adjusted. Having the first section 'in the can' and now to be staying at the comfortable Kichu resort means everyone has a chance to catch their breath.

Jo Juhanson, the technical co-ordinator from Australia, is a gruff but jolly bloke. He has worked on films in New Guinea, Vanuatu and Mexico, as well as Australia (*Babe*, *Chopper* and *The Year My Voice Broke*), and is coping well with the physical rigours, but not so sure about some of the other stuff. He has never met a Rinpoche before, much less worked for one or taken part in a *puja*, and it's all making him a bit nervous.

'You're not into this Buddhist crap, are you?' he asks straight up over breakfast.

I nod timidly.

He shakes his head, clearly disappointed. 'Jeez. If I go home Buddhist, my girlfriend will kill me.'

The Bhutanese crew members, on the other hand, are finding this whole film-making gig to be a wonderful novelty and a social occasion. They are mostly from Thimphu and because the capital is so small, if they aren't personally related, there is a fair chance they at least know of each other. They feel blessed to be working with Rinpoche and delighted to welcome all these foreigners to their country. They are happy and accommodating, no matter what they are asked to do.

The cast is a wonderfully diverse group of people and includes a monk trained in pure mathematics who plays a tractor driver, an official from the Royal Monetary Authority (Bhutan's Reserve Bank), a lieutenant colonel in the King's bodyguard (a giant of a man whose muscular calves are bigger than Kathryn's waist), a BBS (Bhutanese Broadcasting Service) TV reporter with a degree in journalism from the University of California and, in a starring role, a crusty old stall-holder from Thimphu market.

As on *The Cup*, none of the cast has any acting experience. During that shoot, starring mostly Tibetan monks, the average scene required only three takes – which, according to Rinpoche, was a tribute to the powers of concentration from meditation.

In *Travellers & Magicians* the cast are laypeople and each had to audition for their role. Eighteen months before shooting began and when the script was still at draft stage, two Bhutanese sisters, Karma Yangki and Phuntsho Wangmo, started scouring the country for suitable characters. A photo of each possibility was emailed to Rinpoche wherever he was in the world.

Feature film making is almost unheard of in Bhutan. There is a fledgling video industry but it isn't considered glamorous, or even a real job, by the majority of Bhutanese. Often the sisters had to be quite sneaky in their approaches, as when casting the important role of the film's monk. Sonam Kinga, a highly respected Bhutanese scholar, who speaks eight languages and translated Sophocles' play *Antigone* from English to the national language Dzongkha, was hired to translate the play. (Rinpoche had written it in English but wanted to film it in Dzongkha.) The sisters videotaped Sonam Kinga explaining his translations and how he saw the characters, and sent the tape to Rinpoche. In fact, that was his audition – and he passed brilliantly.

Early in 2002, Rinpoche had held auditions in Karma Yangki's lounge room. His annual personal retreat, during which he withdraws from the world to do private meditation practice, interrupted his participation but three months later he came back and did the rest. All the roles were filled except one: Tashi, one of the two male leads. The sisters had been unable to find someone with the special qualities that Rinpoche required and were still looking a fortnight before shooting started.

Finally, Karma Yangki was buying groceries in a shop in Thimphu when a handsome young man with spiky hair and an innocent expression wandered past the window. She hitched up her *kira* and chased him down the street, calling out the character's name, 'Tashi, Tashi!'

When the film is finished, that bewildered young man, Lhakpa Dorji, will be the hottest thing in Bhutan.

Even the extras on the film have special qualities. One morning in Paro, Mal, Kathryn and I arrive at breakfast to find the dining hall full of the most amazing-looking men I have ever seen. They seem massive, though I'm not sure that it's their physical size as much as their imposing presence and wild appearance. They are all stout and dressed in robes, with long greying hair, not unlike North American Indian chiefs. Kathryn squeals with delight at the sight of them while I do my best not to stare. They are incredibly charismatic, which has something to do with the way they hold themselves – relaxed but with great dignity and a kind of contained power. But they are not frightening or intimidating, rather they seem quite jolly.

I think I'm playing it cool, not embarrassing anyone by gawking, when I see Mal is grinning at me. 'It's okay to be impressed,' he whispers. 'They're the *gomchen* here for today's shoot.'

Today's shoot is in a 'magic school' and these men will play the teacher and his students. In real life they are *gomchen*, serious Buddhist practitioners who have spent their lives meditating and studying. But not as monks, rather as lay-people, having their own families and staying within the non-religious world. These half-a-dozen or so men are highly respected for both their learning and their practice. Some are on secondment to the royal family, conducting *puja*s for them.

They are a jovial bunch and enjoy their day of filming, sitting cross-legged on the wooden floor of the centuries-old temple while incense billows about them and the crew runs around adjusting lighting and finetuning camera angles.

※

Every few days the exposed film is sent by DHL courier to Bangkok. There it is processed, matched with sound and made into two tapes. While the original negative stays in Bangkok, stored in a huge refrigerator, one tape is sent to Bhutan to be viewed by the director and crew, the other goes on to Sydney, where the film editors are already at work.

It's John Scott and Lisa-Anne Morris again. Even though it is two months until shooting finishes, the sooner they can immerse themselves in the world of the story, the better. They don't speak Dzongkha (only about 200 000 people in the world do) so each batch of film rushes arrives with a numerical log and notes. They also have a script and it's up to them to figure out what is going on. To me it sounds like an impossible task but Mal assures me they are well up to it. *The Cup* was in Tibetan. Not understanding what the actors are saying is a mere technicality.

The first rushes are brilliant, John tells Mal by telephone, and the crew breathe a collective sigh of relief. It doesn't last. The next telephone call is to say the rushes have gone astray, somewhere between Bangkok and Thimphu, which causes Mal, as producer, some major headaches and frustrates the director and crew, who want to see for themselves how every-thing looks.

John's next call reveals a much bigger problem: the second batch of rushes show damage to the negative, a scratch running through every frame. It can be digitally corrected in post-production and no-one would be the wiser, but that is time-consuming and expensive – not to mention bloody annoying. The crew needs to locate the problem and fix it. Pronto. And they must do it while they are filming, which to me sounds bizarre, but they can't afford to stop production. It must be done on the run.

Meanwhile the big Tata truck due for some forthcoming scenes hasn't turned up, the horse required for a long vigorous galloping scene is off its food and the sound recordist is unable to get out of bed because of a debilitating stomach bug that looks like it may sweep through the crew.

Mal is up to his neck in crises with more looming. He warned me he would be busy but I had no idea. This is my first experience up close with movie-making and it looks seriously stressful. It's a bit like deadline day on a weekly magazine when every minute you are late to the presses costs money. The only difference is Mal faces that pressure every minute of every day. I feel almost guilty that Kathryn and I are having such a lovely, relaxed time. Almost . . .

All the problems must be fixed soon because the Paro section of filming is scheduled to finish and the new location at Chendebji – eight hours' drive away – is nearly built and ready for them to arrive. While the cast and crew are enjoying the warmth and luxury of Kichu resort, the accommodation department is breaking camp and moving it, a mammoth job requiring six huge Tata trucks.

Everything from the camp has to go – beds, bedding, carpets, generators, two whole kitchens, freezers, even the electricity and wiring is stripped out of each room and moved. At the other end a complete camp for more than a hundred people is being painstakingly reassembled.

The cast and crew are reluctant to leave Kichu with its hot showers and soft beds, and I'm starting to wonder about my eagerness to spend the next few months in Thimphu with a family of people I don't know, two of whom, it turns out, are the casting sisters Karma Yangki and Phuntsho Wangmo. After being reunited with Mal, reintroducing him to his daughter and meeting all these interesting people, I am to be dropped off in the middle of the night to live with this extended family of twenty while Mal disappears down some yak trail.

What was I thinking?

'I've known the family for years,' Mal assures me. 'They're lovely people.'

Then you stay with them. How can you leave me and our baby with a bunch of people I've never met?

'I'll be back every seven days or so.'

Seven days? Seven *days! You said three or four . . .*

'You're welcome to come to the next location but it's going to be basic. We're camping, and it'll be cold and wet and pretty miserable. It's not really suitable for a baby.'

So Kathryn and I go to Thimphu.

5

The House of
Many Mothers

It's been a bad night. Kathryn woke six times and, at 4 am, exhausted and in tears, I decide it is time to try the Bhutanese solution for babies who won't sleep. It's off to the temple with her.

Over breakfast I ask Karma Yangki (pronounced *Karma Young-key*), my beautiful, elegant host and newly adopted big sister, if she will take us. 'I need help,' I tell her. 'I'm ready to do it the Bhutanese way.'

She beams a smile full of maternal sympathy and understanding. Aged about thirty-five (she is not sure of her birth date), she is some years younger than me, but as the mother of four children, way ahead in experience.

Over the past few weeks Kathryn and I have been absorbed into Karma Yangki's family in their traditional-style house on the outskirts of the capital city, Thimphu.

Mal has known the family for ten years and stayed in their home a few months ago. Taking snippets from his stories, a dollop from *Lost Horizon* and my own fanciful imaginings, I was expecting a two-storey house with animals – probably cows and sheep – living on the ground floor, with all of us upstairs in one huge room, sleeping sardine-style, by the dying embers of an open fire, which would also be where all the meals were cooked. I imagined I would probably need to use sign language to communicate and everyone would retire early, ready for the next gruelling day of . . . something backbreaking and earthy.

My expectations are wrong in every way.

For one, I don't have to bunk down on the floor with the whole family. That may be the Bhutanese style on farms and in poorer parts of the country, but this family shares a very comfortable home in the nice leafy suburb of Taba, and I have a room all to myself. In fact, it's twice the size of my bedroom in Sydney. The only animals are two playful little terriers and two new kittens. All the members of the family are well educated and speak English, to varying degrees, certainly enough that sign language isn't necessary.

Our host (and husband of Karma Yangki) is Mani Dorji – pronounced *Marnee Dawjee*. He and his brother Tenzin Wangdi turn out to be the emerging Murdochs of Bhutan. They own the largest private press in the country, printing all the school textbooks as well as monastic texts, calendars and business brochures. They own a couple of shops and plan soon to launch the first non-government newspaper. This family's connections reach far and wide throughout the little Himalayan kingdom and it is an extraordinary privilege to be staying with them, and right at the centre of most of what is going on.

The country, a kingdom whose King is also the head of government, is at a most crucial stage in its history as it inches cautiously towards becoming a democracy. Living here I get to meet people involved in drafting the first constitution. The country's most learned men will meet at this home, right where

I eat my lunch each day, to write the country's first official dictionary.

For all that, the family lives quite simply, mostly sleeping on mattresses on the floor, in a warren of rooms downstairs, with their belongings hanging on hooks on the walls. A husband and wife, two of the wife's sisters, a three-year-old and two maids live here, while other sisters, children, cousins, mothers-in-law and more distantly related family come and go. There is another sister in Thimphu, Phuntsho Wangmo, who stays here often, another who lives in east Bhutan, one who studies astrology in Bir, and a brother in Delhi. Keeping track of them all is virtually impossible. Any night of the week the family will pull out another mattress, find some doonas and someone else will become part of the household for a night, a week or longer.

The Bhutanese love a good time and seldom retire before midnight. In the morning I can bump into all sorts of different people who might have slept over. Most baffling of all, sometimes they sleep with the light on.

Kathryn and I rattle around upstairs. On our floor, there is a shrine room, filled with statues of Buddha and *thangkas* (religious paintings), our bedroom, two single bedrooms, a bathroom, a formal lounge room, an open dining area and a large marble verandah with steps down to the driveway. Kathryn has her travel cot set up in one corner of our bedroom, while Mal (when he is here) and I have the double bed and a view across the picturesque rural valley to the snow-capped Himalayas.

The Taba house is a work-in-progress. When Mal stayed here a few months ago during auditions, there was no formal lounge room upstairs or an outside verandah. Karma Yangki got the builders in, told them what she wanted and without plans or any kind of council approval, they did it.

The walls are made of thin pine with no insulation and many gaps, so that there is just one incomplete layer separating us from the sub-zero temperatures outside. The afternoon sun that pours through the glass window warms the room. But the minute it sets, the bitter cold starts seeping through the gaps. By early morning it is so cold that any skin left bare stings.

We wear thermals and hats to bed and sleep under three doonas and two blankets. Kathryn, who would kick off the lightest sheet at home in Australia, wears a zip-up hooded jumpsuit so thickly padded that she can't move her arms and looks like a mini Michelin man. We think she looks cute. She hates it. For a baby who likes to be nude, this clothes-wearing thing is a little tiresome. For once she is overruled.

For me, getting out from under that pile of doonas to face a bucket bath is the hardest part of every day. Washing my hair is even less appealing and drops to once or, at most, twice a week.

Each morning at 8 am Wesel Wangmo (*Yoo-sell Wong-mo*), who at around twenty is the youngest of the family's six sisters, comes and takes Kathryn off for breakfast downstairs. I've brought instant oats and a Bamix to purée vegetables. At nine months she is well into solids and I am religiously following the book on what she should eat. For the first few weeks Wesel Wangmo makes her porridge for breakfast, but once we all start to relax, she has whatever the maids are making for the rest of the family – pumpkin, spinach, even fish soup, with the eyes floating in it, a big favourite with the other children. Kathryn loves it all.

While she is eating breakfast downstairs, the two maids serve me mine in the upstairs dining area. There are usually two or three hot dishes – soup, eggs, vegetables – with pancakes and either sweet Indian tea or salty yak-butter tea. There is enough here for a family of four and if I don't eat plenty, they worry that I don't like their cooking. I try to explain that the feast, laid out before me in a row of beaten copper serving bowls, is somewhat grander than I am used to – two pieces of toast with a smear of Vegemite – but wonderfully appreciated all the same. It is just one of many such conversations we have over the next two months as we dance around each other's cultural differences.

After breakfast I have the top floor virtually to myself while the sisters entertain Kathryn. I can work on my book at the dining table looking out to the road, where the students file past on their way to the nearby school. Or in the formal lounge room. Or sitting up in bed. As golden autumn gives way to frigid winter, I usually opt for working in bed.

I always know exactly where Kathryn is and which sister is playing with her. The thin walls and floor mean her coos of delight and their responses float up to where I am. Sometimes I hear them joining in a chorus of 'Twinkle Twinkle, Little Star' and find myself singing along as I type. When she needs a feed or a nap they bring her back. Otherwise I'm alone with absolutely no excuse not to work.

Kathryn is thriving in this house of many mothers. She sits wherever they put her and plays happily, thrilled to have so much constant attention. She is captivated by Karma Yangki's three-year-old daughter Madonna, who is half-terrified of her. Madonna has never seen such a pale-skinned, redheaded person. It doesn't imbue her with confidence that Kathryn squeals and flaps her arms wildly whenever she walks in the door. It takes a few days but finally Madonna realises how limited Kathryn is – she can't chase her – and becomes intrigued with her odd-looking new playmate.

The family is wonderful and each evening a different sister joins me for dinner. It could be Karma Yangki, the eldest, who as well as being an earth mother has an outrageously rude sense of humour; Karma Chokyi (*Karma Chockie*), aged about twenty-six, who is being courted by her first boy and keeps me up to date with every glorious step of their fledgling romance; Wesel Wangmo, the youngest, who adores Kathryn and is adored back in equal measure; or Phuntsho Wangmo (*Poont-so Wong-mo*), who runs Mal's production office in Thimphu. She is in constant contact with the set and knows all the gossip, like who among the cast and crew might be having a hot affair. It's the sort of stuff that Mal, being a man, never thinks is relevant, and I, of course, find endlessly fascinating.

A conversation with Phuntsho Wangmo is usually juicy and often ends up with me clutching my sides and falling about with hysterics. 'Nooooo! They *didn't.*' 'Oh yes, they did . . . bumped the woman in the next room clean out of her bed . . .'

Dinner could be with any one of the sisters or a combination. I never know who I'm going to get, but whoever it is, I know the conversation is going to be interesting.

꙳

Life in the bosom of this remarkable family should be idyllic, and really it is. Except for the nights.

Kathryn just will not sleep and no matter how entertaining the sisters are and breathtaking the views, it makes little difference to my appreciation of life. I am a walking zombie.

In Sydney she slept. In India she slept. On aeroplanes, rammed under a flickering movie screen, she slept. Strapped to my chest or perched in the backpack she slept. But not here, surrounded by endless beauty and bliss. She wakes every few hours, screaming.

It could be a dozen different things. The cold nights. The dry mountain air causing her to wake up thirsty. The change in food. The change in taste of my breastmilk. The fact the sky is blue or that the day of the week has a 'd' in it. I email friends in Australia for advice but nothing helpful comes back. The drugs they secretly recommend ('I only did this once but, gee, it was good,' two mothers confide) aren't available here.

Kathryn is healthy, eating huge meals and happy during the day but at night we've become locked into a pattern that I need to break. I decide to try a bout of control crying, just like my handbook recommends. It suggests leaving the baby to cry for five minutes before going in and comforting her, then seven or eight minutes and so on, building up the gaps between. It means having nerves of steel and a heart of ice but nevertheless it worked for us in Sydney.

Trying it in Bhutan, where we are sharing a room, means burying my head under the three doonas, two blankets and a pillow, watching the hands move slowly on my luminous watch.

I am just ten minutes into it, while Kathryn is letting loose with both lungs and all the indignance of a healthy, feisty nine-month-old, when I realise someone is pounding on our door.

It is Wesel Wangmo, eyes wide with concern. 'Is Kathryn all right?' she asks, peering anxiously into the room. Karma Yangki, and the other sisters, are worried. It is only 9 pm and, of course, the whole family is still up. I have visions of them all clustered at the foot of the stairs whispering among themselves about what I might be doing to that cute little baby who does nothing but smile at them all day.

The Bhutanese shower their babies with love and attention. When they cry, they pick them up and cuddle them. They can't understand why on earth I would leave her crying. Put it like that and quite frankly, neither can I.

Control crying is not going to work in this household. I give up and take Kathryn into bed with me but I know that is just delaying the problem. Mal will be back in a few days and he takes up most of the double bed. There is hardly room for me, let alone Kathryn. I have to get her to sleep through the night, in her own little bed in her corner of the room.

So I turn to Karma Yangki, fountain of all maternal wisdom. She has told me about the local deity where all the new mothers take their babies. It is the Bhutanese solution for babies who won't sleep. She took her daughter Madonna there and I have witnessed the extraordinary way that child falls asleep. She drops on the spot and, whether it's in her mother's arms or face down on a cold hard floor, she is down for the count.

So after breakfast, Karma Yangki, plus two sisters, two children, Kathryn and myself, pile into the little Maruti (like a small Daihatsu) and head into town to buy offerings to take to the temple. I would leave them my American Express card if

I thought it would help – actually I'd happily hand over Mal in exchange for a good night's sleep. Karma Yangki chuckles at the idea.

On our way to the temple we stop at a general store at one end of the main street. Walking through the streets of Thimphu is like entering the twilight zone. By law the Bhutanese must wear their national dress or they can be stopped by the police and fined. For the women it's the *kira*, a piece of woven fabric that covers the body down to the floor and is held together with a gold brooch at each shoulder. For the men it's a *gho*, which is like a brightly coloured knee-length men's dressing gown with starched white cuffs about twenty centimetres long. The men tie a belt around their waist and bunch up the top half to create a pouch for carrying money, food, even a cup or bowl. Often they stand around with one hand tucked inside, Napoleon-style, managing to look both masculine and dignified. They team the dress with long socks, mostly argyle knit, and leather shoes or sandals. Sometimes they have a slightly distracted air about them, muttering prayers under their breath as they walk.

Thimphu must surely be the world's smallest capital city and the only one without traffic lights. Lights were installed several years ago but the locals considered them unfriendly so got rid of them and reinstated the policeman in an ornate open six-sided gazebo in the middle of the biggest intersection. Wearing white gloves and a blue uniform, he uses a series of elegant and exaggerated hand movements to keep the cars flowing smoothly. The streets are hand-swept and immaculate.

We stop outside a general store where, at Karma Yangki's instruction, I buy a huge brick of butter, three packets of sweet biscuits and the best incense they have. For this the shopkeeper takes me into the back room where the shelves are stocked with row upon row of different types of incense. There must be thirty varieties. I ask Wesel Wangmo for help. She casts an expert eye over it all, has a bit of a chat to the shopkeeper, who is helpful and resplendent in his vivid orange-check *gho*. After much thoughtful discussion and inspection of various incenses, they choose a bundle simply wrapped in handmade paper.

'This is good. It's Bhutanese,' Wesel declares, which I assume means it is superior to Indian.

Just as I'm about to pay, Karma Yangki remembers beer. Black label, she says. Strong. A litre. All together it costs forty-five ngultrim, about A$2.

We pile back into the little Maruti and drive slowly up the valley road to a ridge high above Thimphu. Changangkha Lhakhang is an old fortress-like temple built in the twelfth century. Every baby born in Thimphu Hospital is brought here to be blessed by the local deity, for some reason a male. Another deity resides in another temple on the opposite ridge. That's where you take babies born over that way, Karma Yangki explains.

Looking down onto the city roofs and across the surrounding valley, ringed by snow-covered peaks, the view is breathtaking. Literally. At this altitude, more than 2320 metres above sea level, breathing often can be difficult.

We have gone as far as we can by car and there are hundreds of steep steps to the ancient temple. This is not for the faint-hearted, sleep-deprived or bodily exhausted. Wesel Wangmo takes Kathryn effortlessly while I puff and pant my way to the top. As we climb, mothers with babies tied to their backs pass us coming down. I nod knowingly at them all. *No sleep? Me too. Isn't it the pits?*

We make our way through an elaborate archway, over beaten silver steps, past a stooped old lady who is walking slowly along a line of prayer wheels, spinning each one as she passes, sending prayers and blessings out into the world. Gathered in the courtyard are more old women in colourful *kira*s rapidly counting mantras on their prayer beads, and catching up on the gossip.

Behind wrought-iron grills is a dimly lit chapel with painted walls and a dramatic eleven-head statue of Chenrezig, a particular form of Buddha. On its left is a statue of the local deity, our reason for being here.

A kindly faced young monk suddenly appears, seemingly out of nowhere, and Karma Yangki explains my problem while Kathryn coos and waves her arms with delight. There is something about this dark, musty place that appeals to my baby. The monk takes my offerings and pours the beer into a huge molten candle in front of the statue and lights the bunch of incense, all of it at once, sweeping it through the air sending the smoke in all directions as he mutters and chants in a deep, guttural voice. It's rhythmic and hypnotic. He calls us over and, at Karma Yangki's instruction, I wipe money across Kathryn's head and palms, and give it to the monk. He taps her on the head with a sacred relic wrapped in silk, then pours special water into my palm. I drink it and wipe the rest over Kathryn's head. He smiles and we are done.

We retrace the hundreds of steps down to the car and then it's back to the family's office headquarters for pizza. *Pizza?* The sisters laugh at the look on my face, particularly when after twenty minutes, two large square pizza boxes arrive at the office.

※

Just when I think I am starting to get a handle on Bhutan, whenever I think I've got it figured, something comes along to make me realise I understand nothing. This country is a bewildering paradox all its own.

Bhutanese culture has developed mostly independently of outside influences. It has a population of less than a million and yet shares borders with two of the most densely populated countries on earth, China and India.

In 1996 the King decreed that in line with the people's Buddhist philosophy, Gross National Happiness would be more important than Gross National Product. 'Most socioeconomic indicators are an attempt at measuring means; they do not measure ends,' he said.

The Bhutanese believe that it is essential that development benefits the economic, social, emotional, spiritual and cultural needs of the people. As they cautiously move towards a democracy, every step is evaluated to ensure that it leads both directly and indirectly to happiness, not just more development.

One result is that while the rest of the world argues about it, forest cover in Bhutan is increasing rather than decreasing. It is by royal decree that sixty per cent of the land stays as forest cover at all times. Every Bhutanese citizen is allowed to cut down one tree each year but must replace it by replanting two trees. Managing their growing prosperity and democratisation is a constant topic of discussion in the 'office', where we enjoy our takeaway pizzas.

This little network of rooms tucked behind two shops is where it all happens. Mani Dorji runs the family businesses from here. It also doubles as the production office for Rinpoche's film company, Prayer Flag Pictures, and everywhere are boxes marked *Travellers & Magicians* containing stray film equipment and props. An endless stream of visitors drop by for business or a chat. The telephone rings constantly. Phuntsho Wangmo and her four-year-old daughter Renee mostly live in two sparsely furnished rooms above the office, accessible by a steep ladder, while her husband Tenzin Wangdi lives mostly in the border town of Phuntsoling.

The live-in maid brings us sweet tea to go with our pizzas. It is a feast. While we lick melted cheese and fried onion off our fingers, an uncle drops by and immediately the discussion turns to the soaring property prices in Thimphu. I feel right at home. This could be any office in Australia. Clearly the obsession with the price of real estate is universal.

The sisters shake their heads and marvel at how big and cosmpolitan Thimphu is becoming. Demand for homes far outstrips supply, and real estate in some places has quadrupled in value over the past few years.

Taba, where my hosts Karma Yangki and Mani Dorji live, is a new middle-class suburb on the outskirts of town, along the Wang Chhu River. Phuntsho Wangmo and her husband have bought land nearby and plan to build a home there in a few years. Or that was their plan until they discovered that the government had moved it. The land they thought they'd bought was nicely positioned in the verdant valley. The land they actually have been given has shifted up the hill. American town planners advised on the subdivision and recommended creating a green space. So the government took back from the buyers thirty per cent of the land to create parks, which meant moving the plots around. Phuntsho Wangmo is happy about green space but would prefer that each landowner agree to provide gardens on their own property, and is writing to the powers that be.

The conversation moves on to personal income tax, which, just last year, the Bhutanese were asked to pay for the first time. Most of the rural population earns less than the tax threshold of 100 000 ngultrim (about A$4000) and so are exempt.

It seems typically Bhutanese that the way the government introduced it was just to ask nicely for everyone who earns an income to register. Presumably they have, though it's too soon to know for sure. I gather from the conversation around me that no-one begrudges it. The way they see it, a big city like Thimphu needs the sort of infrastructure and services only national taxes could provide.

It is only recently that Thimphu started a daily garbage collection. Small, modern, clean and shiny compacter trucks, donated by Japan, tour the city and suburbs each morning. Sounding like Mr Whippy vans, they play music (the Bhutanese equivalent of 'Greensleeves') as they cruise the streets. The women run out and toss their boxes and scraps into the back. Plastic bags are a rarity because of the threat they pose to the environment and the Bhutanese seldom use them.

Chooing, an energetic young woman in her twenties who works on the film as talent co-ordinator, told me how she and her friends spend their spare time collecting garbage from the outlying areas that the trucks don't yet service. They drive around in their own cars, piling the rubbish into the boot. Such is the spirit of generosity that permeates this delightful country.

After lunch Kathryn and I leave the sisters and their uncle to catch up on Thimphu news and we take a taxi back to the family home at Taba. The maid spots us coming down the driveway and immediately starts boiling milk for our sweetened tea. But before it is ready we've passed out together on the bed and both sleep solidly for three hours.

Already the God of Nod is doing his stuff and I am feeling hopeful for the night ahead.

❋

We get off to a good start – Kathryn is asleep by 8 pm and still not a peep out of her by midnight when the maids unroll their mats on the floor in the downstairs living room, signalling that the household is turning in.

We make it till 2.10 am and then Kathryn wakes, screaming so loudly I am sure Mal will hear her 150 kilometres away. I pop my head up every now and then to soothe her then slide back under my three doonas, two blankets and a pillow, eventually joining in her tears. I keep an ear out for a knock on the door, but it doesn't come. Finally at 3.45 am she falls asleep. In the morning I am embarrassed, guilty, shy, coy, ashamed and horrified. What must the family think?

Wesel Wangmo comes in, smiling and cheery as always, to take Kathryn for her breakfast. The two of them coo with delight at the sight of each other.

'I hope we didn't wake anyone last night,' I venture. 'Kathryn cried a little bit.'

Wesel Wangmo smiles and shakes her head. No-one heard a thing. Or if they did they are way too kind to let me know.

Tonight Kathryn does sleep. All night. Right through. And so do I. Nine glorious, uninterrupted hours. Perky? After that much sleep, I feel like a teenager again. And she pretty much sleeps through every night thereafter. The God of Nod has worked his magic. So it has taken forty-eight hours for the offerings to work. Pah! I'm a believer. No matter where you are, a good night's sleep is the very best kind of miracle.

6

Oh Glorious Luminosity

For the first few weeks I struggle to get my mouth around the sisters' names. It's easy enough for Mal, who has known the family for years, and they just roll off his tongue. After delivering us here, he stayed for the first few days, being needed in the Thimphu office. But then he was off up the yak trail, leaving me on my own with my hosts.

I manage for a while to get by without actually uttering anyone's name, but I realise I can't continue to live under their roof this way.

The Bhutanese have about fifty names which they mix and match. There is no logical reason as to why some people use two names and others only one, but all the sisters use two. Nor do their names bear any relation to their marital status, gender or family affiliations. So there is no point in trying to make any sense of them.

When I find out the English translations of their names, I'm dumbfounded. Before, I was nervous about mispronouncing them, now I'm completely intimidated about speaking to these exalted people at all.

The eldest sister is Karma Yangki, which means 'Activity of Spaciousness'. The next sister is Phuntsho Wangmo, 'Powerful Mother of Excellent Abundance'. Beautiful Karma Chokyi is 'Activity of the Dharma'. And Wesel Wangmo, the kind, loving sister who looks after Kathryn most of the time, is 'Powerful Mother of Luminosity'. According to the *Australian Women's Weekly Book of Names*, Bunty means 'pet lamb'. It just doesn't compare.

For a few days I try thinking of the women in these terms.

Good morning Activity of Spaciousness, isn't it a beautiful morning?

Good afternoon Powerful Mother of Luminosity, how's Kathryn's nappy rash?

It transforms every exchange into something verging on the divine.

In Bhutan it is traditional for lamas to name babies, and Mal has been there when new parents have presented their baby to Rinpoche, seeking both his blessing and a name. Usually Rinpoche looks around his attendants and selects a hybrid of their names. On one occasion he looked around, spotted Mal and told the new parents 'Mal Watson'. According to people who were there at the time, the parents were unable to hide their horror. Seeing their distress, Rinpoche relented and gave them something more Bhutanese.

But Rinpoche broke with tradition when he named the Taba children. Karma Yangki's three-year-old daughter is Madonna, after the singer, and Phuntsho Wangmo's four-year-old daughter is called Renee, after one of his Canadian students.

❊

It starts to turn ever colder. Breakfast is icy, while lunch is glorious, with the sun pouring through the glass windows on the first floor. Dinner is laid out for me in the formal lounge room upstairs and it is cosy if I remember to draw the curtains and turn on the heaters early enough to warm the room.

Eight couches, two- and three-seaters covered in matching beige embossed fabric, stand against the walls. In front of each is a traditional Bhutanese table – low and orange with carved, brightly painted dragons. The maids cover one with a row of beaten copper serving dishes. While I eat with whichever sister I have for company for the evening, the rest of the family and whoever is around eat downstairs. It is not usually a formal affair. Rather than sitting down together in one spot, bowls are lined along the kitchen bench and they help themselves when they feel like it, taking the food back to their own room, sitting around on the floor, or standing at the kitchen bench.

The food is fresh, varied and always good. The maids prepare the meals under Karma Yangki's instructions, though she is just as likely to be working alongside them, elbow deep in *momo* dough or peeling potatoes.

Today is Friday, the first day of the weekend market when the food brought in from the villages is at its freshest and most expensive. Karma Yangki is always there early, arguing with the stall-holders, poking and prodding all their vegetables. The little table in front of me groans with the weight of all the dishes. Tonight is an even bigger feast than usual. Red rice (a Bhutanese speciality, but gaining popularity in health food shops around the world), deep-fried eggs (first hard-boiled, shelled, then dipped in batter – sensational), riverweed soup, boiled meat, a couple of vegetable dishes and a plate of cucumber slices (which have been popping up at every meal since I mentioned how big and juicy I thought they were).

The two maids, who don't speak English, add to the table a pile of plates and a tray of glasses with bottled water. I realise I must be expecting more than just one sister. After a few minutes, all the sisters join me. This really is a treat. Mani Dorji is working late, bidding for a large printing contract while Phuntsho Wangmo's husband Tenzin Wangdi (business partner and brother of Mani Dorji) is in Switzerland receiving an international award recognising their excellence in business. So tonight it's just us girls. We leave our shoes at the door – my flat ones and their impossibly high wedges. Bhutanese women are petite and love the extra height that high heels give them.

While the lounge room is cosy, the bare floorboards are cold and I sit on a couch with my feet tucked under me, but Karma Yangki and Phuntsho Wangmo take up their favoured positions cross-legged on the floor. Madonna and Renee come in and out, listen to us talk, get bored, tease each other, run out, listen outside my bedroom door in case Kathryn is awake and ready to play, then give up and come back in. Finally exhausted, they fall asleep half on the bare floor and half on their mothers' laps.

The two younger sisters sit on couches. They sometimes contribute to the conversation but in deference to their older sisters, mainly they sit back and listen.

Bhutanese women generally have ribald senses of humour and are not the least bit prudish. The whole country, it seems, shares an obsession with penises. Larger-than-life wooden phalluses hang from house eaves in every village. Some of them are ornately carved and so huge that they require four men to lift them into place. They also appear beautifully painted on the outside of homes, proudly displayed and openly admired.

On one level, the phallus is considered a sign of power and is intended to ward off evil spirits. On another, it is meant to represent the human form, with its inherent wisdom, as an antidote to ego, the source of all one's suffering. Phalluses are attached to roofs along with a dagger, representing opposite impulses. Each is meant to counteract the energy of the other, leading to the calming of one's mind.

❋

The women openly joke about sex and nothing seems to shock them. But don't be fooled, a sophisticated, western-educated Bhutanese man warned me: 'A westerner might think from the way that they speak that they are experienced and willing, but that is not the case. They are all talk. A western man will get a shock if he misinterprets their conversation for what they might do.' Living with them I discover this to be true. They can be downright bawdy and laugh about things that would make my genteel mother-in-law blush. But they aren't at all promiscuous, their dress and behaviour is demure and the protocols of dating are positively Victorian.

Karma Yangki is renowned within the family for her rude sense of humour and, in particular, her skilful double entendre. She often has the other sisters in hysterics. Unfortunately the play on words doesn't always work in English and even with an explanation I am left mystified as to why they are falling about on the floor clutching their sides.

But while the word plays don't always translate, the humour generally does, and we share much laughter. They can be terribly dry and love to tease and be teased. They are as curious about my social mores as I am about theirs, and we have many fascinating exchanges. Some make me feel inspired and delightfully connected, others leave me feeling completely gobsmacked, like we are from different planets. Tonight's conversation about childbirth is one of those times.

The older married sisters tell me about their Bhutanese maid who went into labour here at Taba one day. It lasted twelve hours. 'Twelve hours,' say Karma Yangki and Phuntsho Wangmo in awed tones, looking at each other and shaking their heads. The maid screamed so much that they didn't know what to do. I nod blankly. Twelve hours of screaming sounds kind of normal. I wait for a punchline but it doesn't come.

I respond with my most extraordinary birth story, the Tibetan woman I met in Canada who popped hers out while weaving. Five children, just two hours of labour each. 'Two hours,' I say in my best awed tone. It is their turn to look blank and I guess they're waiting for my punchline.

It turns out that Karma Yangki popped hers out in half an hour. Four babies, half an hour each. (Her other three daughters live with Mani Dorji's sister in the royal compound, partly because it is nearer to their school and also because of the organic nature of relationships between the Bhutanese. Raising each other's children is quite common.)

The sisters had been shocked (and appalled, I suspect) by the maid who carried on and on making so much noise and took forever. And they were completely nonplussed by my story of the Tibetan woman.

They ask about my experience with childbirth.

I admit that mine was like the maid's, except that I had drugs. I add that Mal was there for the whole ten hours, taking Kathryn in his arms the instant she appeared. The first voice she heard was his, whispering quietly in her ear.

I don't know what they make of this but it is obviously something because they start to talk rapidly between themselves without translating, which is very rare. Childbirth and bringing up babies is women's work but they seem delighted at how much Mal engages with Kathryn, changing nappies and doing whatever else is required.

※

On the walls around us in the lounge room hang Buddhist *thangka*s and photos of the four Kings of Bhutan. The monarchy is only in its fourth generation and credited with bringing peace and harmony to the troubled country.

The current monarch, His Majesty King Jigme Singye Wangchuck, is incredibly handsome, in an old-fashioned, movie-matinee-idol kind of way. He has the feline eyes and high cheekbones of the northern Bhutanese, with a piercing gaze and a sensual mouth. In the photo he wears an orange and yellow checked *gho*, the colours of the Bhutanese flag. I have seen the same photo on walls in shops, homes and public places.

The reverence and love the Bhutanese feel for their King is nothing short of astonishing. Well, it is to me, coming from the west and used to the ongoing scandals of Britain's Windsor family, which are duly reported from one side of the world to the other. King Jigme Singye Wangchuck is as far from that as could be possible.

The *Druk Gyalpo*, Precious Ruler of the Dragon People, was educated in English boarding schools but now virtually never leaves Bhutan, being far too busy working for his people. He is both regal and humble. His royal palace is simple and his office just a log cabin in the verdant, pine-covered hills above Thimphu. His attendants, in keeping with tradition, walk barefoot.

As King he is also head of government but the country is in the process of becoming a democracy and currently drafting its first constitution. He is the driving force, happily lessening his own executive power.

But what makes the King truly stand apart from other leaders is his attitude, which encompasses a breadth and depth of vision and responsibility not often seen anywhere in the world. His philosophy of Gross National Happiness has earned him respect among leaders all over the world.

Mieko Nishimizu of the World Bank said at the time of the King's Silver Jubilee in 1999:

> It is rare to find a nation, today or in the history of our globe, whose people share a clear and dynamic vision rooted in their cultural heritage and common values. It is even rarer to encounter a nation which, by the strength of her conviction, initiates a new paradigm for the transformation of its society . . . that challenges the world to reconsider established methods of measuring change. This unique nation is the Kingdom of Bhutan and the ultimate source of its uniqueness rests singularly in the leadership of His Majesty.

Not surprisingly, when the sisters talk about their King it is with great reverence and respect. He is an extraordinary man doing great things for their country.

He also has four wives. This little detail is passed over so quickly that when I'm told, I'm not sure I heard correctly.

'Four wives?'

'Oh yes,' they nod. 'They're sisters.'

'The King married four sisters?'

They smile at my naivety. I did buy a book on Bhutan before I left Australia but with a baby and a looming book deadline, I'm ashamed to admit I never actually opened it. It's still in its wrapping in my suitcase.

They nod but will say no more. The royal family is not a topic for idle gossip. I find out from a smattering of other sources that the King married the four sisters in one huge wedding spectacular in 1988 in front of hundreds of monks and abbots.

The four Queens are all stunningly beautiful, accomplished and each has her own projects aimed at improving the wellbeing of their people, including child welfare, AIDS prevention, education and women's rights.

Marrying four sisters is not so unusual in Bhutan. It is quite common in the poorer rural communities where one bride will marry a family of brothers, or one groom will marry all the sisters. It makes economic sense to set up just one household and also it saves carving up the family farm.

The King obviously didn't have such economic concerns. But it explains why the Bhutanese don't see his multiple marriage as unusual.

His Majesty had been living with the four sisters for ten years – and had two princes – before he married them. This also isn't considered much of a big deal. Ironically, while the marriage rate declines in the west, formal weddings are a relatively new phenomenon in Bhutan, copied from their Indian neighbours and pursued only by very modern, middle-class couples.

Traditionally marriages occur when a couple decide they want to be married. If they agree, then that's it. They are husband and wife.

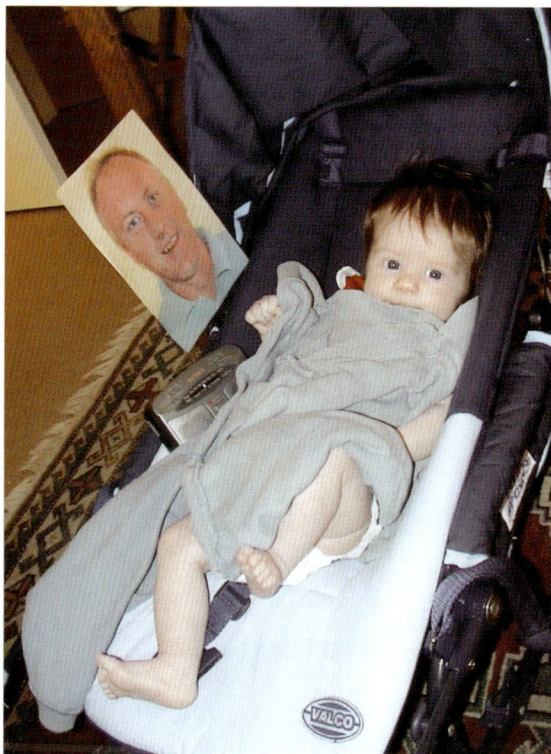

Kathryn with Daddy-on-a-stick, his smelly T-shirt and the tape of his voice.

Mal and I with Kathryn and all her devoted Muncles at the *labrang* in Bir.

Sonam Choepel and Ugyen Thrinley play with Kathryn, the 'glow in the dark' baby.

Wesel Wangmo, Karma Yangki and Karma Chokyi outside their Taba home. Behind them is their famous verandah.

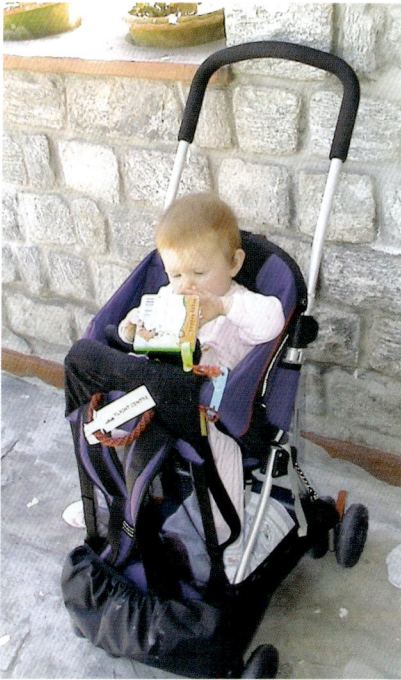

Kathryn in the high-tech pram
that converts into a backpack.

Karma Yangki's mother-in-law
outside her front door.

The magnificent Thimphu *dzong*, built without a single nail.

Khyentse Norbu directs a scene for *Travellers & Magicians* at the now famous rock face with the painting of Guru Rinpoche. The 'apple man' sits in the foreground. (Photo by Rasa Bahls, © Prayer Flag Pictures, 2003)

Khyentse Norbu directs the *gomchen* in the 'magic house'. (Photo by Rasa Bahls, © Prayer Flag Pictures, 2003)

Kathryn's favourite place – in a sling on Mal's chest.

Karma Chokyi (left) and her friends, dressed in their school *kira*s, play with Kathryn after classes.

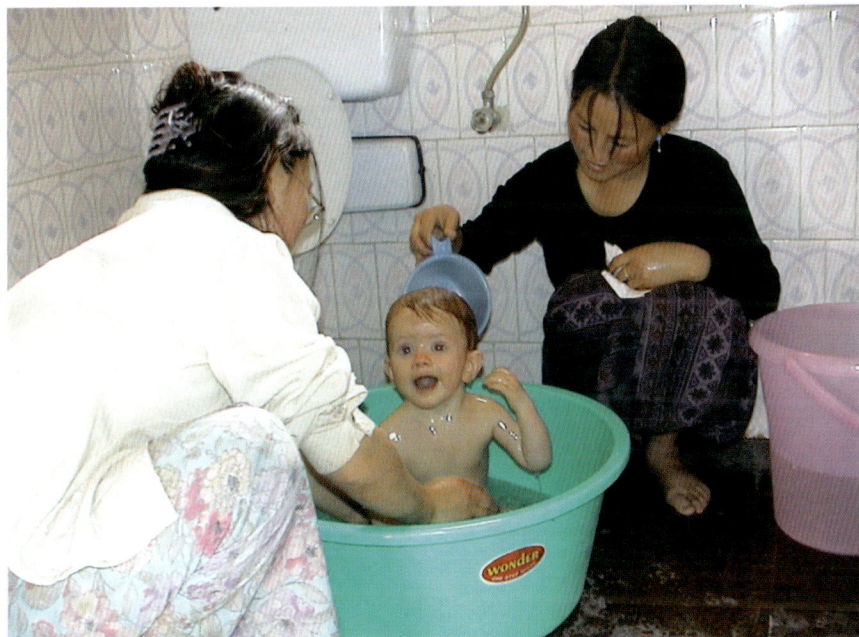

Wesel Wangmo and Karma Chokyi bathe Kathryn in a bucket.

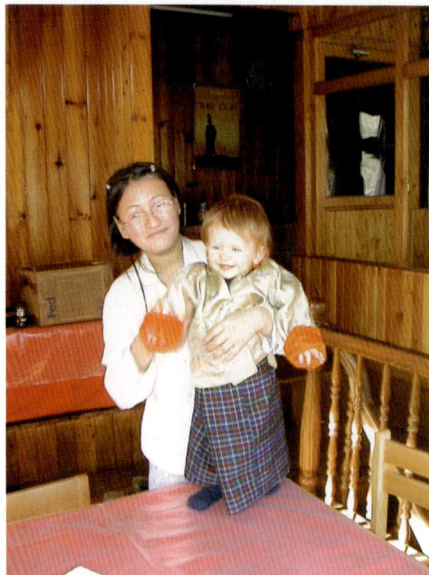

Wesel Wangmo dresses Kathryn in a *kira* for the day.

Madonna, Karma Yangki and Kathryn take a walk along the beautiful Wang Chhu River near the Queen Mother's palace, on the outskirts of Taba.

Ten of the eminent and learned men who created Bhutan's first official dictionary. The very important and kindly Lungtaen Gyatsho is wearing robes and standing in the middle of the back row. (Photo courtesy of *The Kuensel*)

At the wrap party: me, Kathryn, Karma Yangki, Phuntsho Wangmo and Wesel Wangmo.

Mal and I take Kathryn to receive a blessing from Khandro Tsering Chodron, one of the greatest female Buddhist practitioners of our time.

After an auspicious visit to Khandro, a very happy Mal and Kathryn pose outside the royal palace in Gangtok.

Dressed in *kira*s for the royal premiere of *Travellers & Magicians*.

Moments before the arrival of the four Queens of Bhutan at the royal premiere, Kathryn chases Mal down the red carpet screaming 'Daddy, Daddy!'

The farewell dinner. Front row: Karma Chokyi, Kathryn, Wesel Wangmo and Renee. Middle row: me, Phuntsho Wangmo, Mani Dorji, Karma Yangki and Madonna. Mal stands at the back.

The talk moves on to someone the sisters know who has taken a second wife. They explain that it is perfectly acceptable in Bhutanese society as long as the first wife agrees. Human relationships here are as complicated and convoluted as anywhere and the women are as intrigued as I am by the dynamics that must go on within the household.

Karma Yangki and Phuntsho Wangmo admit they wouldn't be happy if their husbands brought home another wife. It doesn't cause them undue concern because, they say, their husbands just aren't like that. They ask about Mal. I explain that we aren't married and he would be free to bring home another woman . . . but that if he did I would be gone and I might just kill him on my way out the door. They nod emphatically. 'Same, same,' they say and we all laugh.

I ask if they are ever tempted to take another husband and they fall about laughing. Of course it's possible but who would want two husbands? We shake our heads furiously. Same, same.

It seems the Bhutanese are not so worried about rules, and their relationships stay amazingly fluid. The crucial thing is that people don't get hurt. That's much more important than adhering to some sort of socially acceptable mode of behaviour. The sisters don't sit in judgment on anyone. It's just not their way. Karma Yangki mentions a woman in Thimphu who some married men visit. She calls her 'the mistress'. She has a nice home, cooks a nice meal, makes a fuss of the men and probably sleeps with them. Karma Yangki shrugs. Why should that bother anybody?

Rinpoche says the Bhutanese share a lack of inhibition, which is refreshing: 'The non-existence of such inhibition can be a blessing. Other cultures have lost this sense of freedom or openness, in turn possibly making them into sexually repressed societies. So-called sophistication may have made their minds narrow and rigid, depriving them of a source of happiness. Unfortunately, Bhutanese may be learning to have that self-consciousness.'

Divorce, it seems, is also pretty fluid. Should a couple decide to split, they just go their separate ways. There are laws to ensure a father continues to support his child.

In poorer rural communities, where often everybody lives and sleeps together in one room, courtships can be especially brief – sometimes just a pre-arranged knock on the window in the middle of the night, while the rest of the family pretends not to notice. There is no shame attached to such dalliances.

It's nice if the man is still there in the morning and the relationship continues, but no shame to the woman if his intentions turn out to be only short term. As a result there are many single mothers bringing up children in the villages. But rather than stigmatise them, the community gathers around to help.

※

The Queens each have their own palace in the forest-covered hills overlooking Thimphu, and the King maintains his own palace, which is close to them all. How they co-ordinate the marital visits is anyone's guess and not the sort of thing the sisters are likely to speculate about. I give myself a mental slap and remind myself I am not here for *New Idea*.

The extended royal family includes the much-loved Queen Mother (who has her own palace at the other end of Thimphu Valley), the Crown Prince, seven young Princesses, the King's four sisters and his three aunts, also Princesses. Should you wish to contact any members of the royal family, their personal phone numbers are listed in the front of the telephone book. I guess the Bhutanese don't make crank calls.

I gather from the way the sisters speak about the Royals that one's standing in Thimphu society has a lot to do with how close one is to the royal court. But it isn't just about social standing. The people genuinely revere their King. Apart from his achievements as a visionary ruler he is renowned as an accomplished Buddhist practitioner.

The other walls of the room carry a black-and-white photo of the previous three monarchs, looking dashing and dignified, and wearing ever-more elaborate hats. The first King was enthroned in 1907, after a bloody period of civil wars within the country and threats from outside, including violent skirmishes with British troops on the Indian side and the growing influence of China on the Tibetan side. Ugyen Wangchuck was a young but powerful regional leader who developed close relations with the British. He accompanied explorer Francis Younghusband when he invaded Tibet in 1904 and helped negotiate the treaty between Britain and Tibet.

When the secular ruler of Bhutan died in 1907, Ugyen Wangchuck was elected unanimously by the country's chiefs and principal lamas, and installed as the first hereditary monarch, the *Druk Gyalpo*, Dragon King. (While Wangchuk is a common name in Bhutan, the royal family is differentiated by the spelling. They are Wangchuck, with an extra 'c'.)

It seems strange to me that more than 100 years after France got rid of its royal family, Bhutan was creating one. The sisters shake their heads. They don't find it strange at all. Since their inception, Phuntsho Wangmo tells me, the royal family has introduced an era of unprecedented stability and peace.

※

The two younger sisters listen to everything that is being discussed but say little. Wesel Wangmo is quite studious, carrying with her a scrapbook of cuttings about His Holiness the Dalai Lama. Her manner is often reserved, so I'm not surprised by her silence. But it seems unlike Karma Chokyi, who loves to chat. When we have dinner she talks constantly — about school, her friends, her family, what she wants to do with her life. To see her so restrained in the presence of her elders is more surprising.

Karma Chokyi thinks she is about twenty-six but is not too sure. Her mother is a bit vague about her birthday and none of the sisters can agree. This causes huge frustration for Karma Chokyi. One of the middle two sisters, Pema Bidha (*Pema Bidder*), is doing an intensive seven-year degree course in Tibetan astrology at an Indian university and Karma Chokyi would love to have her chart done.

'Mum tells me to stop asking. She says she had seven children and can't be expected to remember the birthdays of everyone. I asked my sisters and one remembers it being in summer and another in winter.'

Sometimes she reads all the star signs in the Indian magazines that sell in Thimphu and tries to recognise herself in one of the twelve personalities described.

Karma Chokyi, still at school but dreaming of her life after graduation, is misty-eyed and enjoying her first romance. She tells me she likes the Indian idea of marriage, which, like her friends, she has seen in Hindi movies. Indians throw huge wedding ceremonies – the bride wearing an elaborate red and gold sari with lots of jewellery while the man wears a suit and often rides to the ceremony on a white horse. The parties are legendary and, for the really rich families, can go on for days. Some modern Bhutanese couples have chosen to celebrate their union in the Indian manner and Karma Chokyi says it is a custom she too would like to adopt. When the time comes, she adds coyly.

She is a beautiful young woman, with long black hair that falls past her waist in a most un-Bhutanese fashion. Traditionally they wear it in a short angular cropped bob with a fringe. It's strange to my untrained eye that the women in the fields wear these short, modern-looking haircuts while Karma Yangki and Karma Chokyi's style, more typical of Asian women, is actually considered quite radical. Karma Chokyi is sweet-natured, always smiling and vibrant, with lots to say, although she tells me she gets completely tongue-tied with boys who aren't her cousins or schoolmates.

One night shortly after I arrived she revealed she would like to be a fashion designer. I couldn't have been more surprised if she said she wanted to be a train driver. In Bhutan the women have one dress style: the *kira*. It's thousands of years old and they are fiercely proud of it. It is worn by the poorest peasant in the field, by the elegant Queens at state functions, and everywhere in between. At home the wealthier women might occasionally wear western-style clothes that have come across the border from India or China, but in public it is always the *kira*. It's the law – and a matter of pride.

I asked if Karma Chokyi meant she wanted to be a *fabric* designer, creating new designs of cloth for the *kira*. 'No,' she said, shaking her head emphatically. 'I want to design fashion.'

She disappeared downstairs and returned with a folder, which she shyly pushed across the table. Inside were the most beautifully drawn sketches, each one a work of art. The female figures were elegant and lightly shaded, giving a hint of their form. But it is what they were wearing that left me speechless.

A traditional *kira* is floor length and pinned high on the shoulder, worn with an undershirt that has sleeves that extend beyond the fingertips. Barely a millimetre of womanly flesh is exposed. Since arriving in Bhutan I had not so much as glimpsed a female ankle. Karma Chokyi's designs showed off bare shoulders and midriffs, with hems that were thigh high. The amount of flesh on display would be at home in an Australian nightclub or on a beach.

The highly original designs used the traditional woven *kira* cloth in sexy stylish body-hugging dresses with slashes of fabric and detail. They were utterly fabulous and, ironically, couldn't be less appropriate in this country. And therein lies her frustration: Karma Chokyi would love to pursue a career in fashion but she doesn't want to leave Bhutan. As modern and progressive as she is, the pull of the outside world is not strong enough to make her want to leave her family or this unique little kingdom, with all its charm and eccentricities.

I hear the same from Karma Yogini, her cousin and best friend. The two bright, young twenty-somethings are planning a big celebratory holiday when they finally finish their end-of-year exams in a few months – and where are they going? Perhaps over the border to cosmopolitan Mumbai to go shopping, see lots of movies and hang out with other young groovy people their age? No. They are very excited about going back to their remote family village and spending time with their poor and elderly grandmother, helping on the farm and sleeping on the bare floor of her traditional Bhutanese home.

Such are the priorities of the very delightful Karma Chokyi. And the man lucky enough to be courting her is the doctor on Rinpoche's film, an earnest, handsome man in his early thirties, called Dr Thinley Norbu.

It was a condition of the Americans on the crew that the production have a doctor of western medicine on set at all times. Enter Dr Thinley Norbu, who trained in India and spends most of the film handing out pills to the foreigners for upset stomachs. From the moment he was hired, he was destined to meet Karma Chokyi. Her family has been involved in every aspect of the film since it was nothing more than a first draft. Karma Yangki and husband Mani Dorji have small on-screen roles. Their cousin Karma Loday is a purchasing officer. Phuntsho Wangmo works with Mal. And an aunt, Phuntsho Dolma, works in the make-up department.

At a Thimphu party during filming, Phuntsho Dolma notices the nice film doctor is single and good-looking – perfect for her niece. When the good doctor announces his intention to leave the party, the aunt declares he must drop Karma Chokyi home. Taba is not exactly on his way and everyone knows immediately what she has in mind. Karma Chokyi is consumed with embarrassment but wouldn't dream of disobeying a family elder; Dr Thinley is way too polite and well mannered to refuse such a request. And so the scene for romance is set. He drives Karma Chokyi home.

The next day I ask her whether the doctor is handsome. She tells me she doesn't know what he looks like because she sat in the back seat of his little Maruti and didn't dare look at him.

It doesn't matter. Dr Thinley obviously did get a peek at his coy charge in the back seat and is smitten. He telephones three times the next day, just to say hello. He is an ardent suitor and Karma Chokyi has never experienced anything like it. She is completely atwitter, blushing whenever the telephone rings. It is so lovely. I don't think I could enjoy this romance any more if I was having it myself.

After a few days of telephone calls, Dr Thinley invites her on their first date – a walk in the park. Karma Chokyi seeks permission from her elder sister and then accepts.

The date is very Bhutanese. When Dr Thinley turns up, all polished and scrubbed and combed, wearing a neatly pressed *gho* and a grin from ear to ear, he is greeted by Karma Chokyi and two giggling cousins. They are coming along too.

He seems not the least bit fussed. The four pile into the little car while Wesel Wangmo, the two maids, Kathryn and I stand on the verandah, waving. The cousins are giggling so much I fear they will self-combust, while Karma Chokyi is the colour of the chillies drying on the roof, but clearly enjoying every minute.

I remember when boys would come to pick up my older sister, I was banished to my bedroom for fear I might embarrass her in front of a boy. That wouldn't occur to Karma Chokyi. The dating ritual here is much more formal and yet, in some ways, more relaxed. Her family couldn't embarrass her. The onus is entirely on him. If they don't like him, he wouldn't get inside the door.

They drop the cousins at their home and on the way back to Taba, finally alone, stop at the park. It's too cold to walk so they sit in the car and talk.

Dr Thinley is clearly very keen and mentions the word 'marriage'. Karma Chokyi is both delighted and terrified. She's only just looked this man in the face and already he is talking this way. It is not a proposal, rather he wants to know if she thinks she could see him in that light. She demurs.

'Too soon,' she tells him.

'Think about it,' he says.

Over the next two weeks Dr Thinley becomes a regular appendage to life at Taba. While Karma Chokyi asks him to leave her alone so she can study for her final exams, he agrees then disregards her request. When he isn't dropping in, apparently on the way somewhere (Taba is on the outskirts of Thimphu, making that unlikely), he is ringing on the telephone.

Karma Chokyi can't decide if she is romantically attracted to him or not but certainly is enjoying the attention. While she thinks about this, the relationship moves into the next crucial stage – which has nothing to do with Karma Chokyi and everything to do with the family. Before it can go any further they must give their approval. Suddenly Dr Thinley is everywhere, joining in everything, while Karma Chokyi is nowhere to be seen. It is like he is dating the older sisters. He drives Karma Yangki to the market, has tea with us upstairs in the formal lounge room, and takes Karma Yangki, Wesel Wangmo, Kathryn and myself on a photographic tour of Thimphu.

Over dinner one night Karma Chokyi tells me she wouldn't dream of having a relationship with a man that her family didn't like. She owes them everything, she says. Elder sister Karma Yangki provides the roof over her head, her food and many other kindnesses. So she is content to wait, let the family get to know him, and see what they say.

I can't imagine beautiful, generous-hearted Karma Yangki not liking anyone. I ask her, expecting an enthusiastic response. But she demurs.

'Too soon,' she says.

Their mother is alive and a frequent visitor to the home, but Karma Yangki has assumed the unofficial role of guardian to her little sister and she takes it very seriously. She doesn't know Dr Thinley nearly well enough to give her blessing. While she makes up her mind, Dr Thinley is absorbed into family life, albeit on his best behaviour.

7

The Beast and the Oracle

The sisters seek advice on the budding romance from an unusual source – an oracle, or shaman. And not just any shaman, but one whose powers of clairvoyance are legendary throughout Bhutan. The royal family seek out this woman as do high lamas.

Karma Yangki invites me along. Would I like to come for a visit with a shaman? Hello? I can't believe my luck. I didn't work in women's magazines for all those years not to have developed an overactive interest in such things. I'm purple with excitement.

It takes a while to organise as the shaman is in eastern Bhutan on business. Each day for three weeks I wonder if this will be the day. I've almost given up when finally one morning Karma Yangki's head bobs up above the stairway bannister while I'm eating breakfast.

It's today. The shaman is home. We're on. She flashes a grin and disappears.

After breakfast, five of us pile into the little green Maruti – Karma Yangki, Phuntsho Wangmo, Karma Chokyi, Kathryn and me. It's hard to tell who is the most excited. We're a merry lot, laughing and chatting as we go.

Phuntsho Wangmo explains how the shaman works. She reads faces and can tell things just from looking at you, but if you have something specific then she is happy to answer questions. I say I would like to know about my books and Kathryn. Nothing specific. Anything really. I'm just along for the ride.

Our hour-long trip takes us away from Thimphu, past Karma Chokyi's high school, across beautiful Wang Chhu River on a small suspension bridge draped in prayer flags, alongside the high walls of the Queen Mother's palace, past a military training headquarters and through a couple of towns where the soldiers' families live. Then it's up a steep hill. Up and up we climb. It's so sheer that Phuntsho Wangmo stalls a few times and we breathe in. I don't know why, but we all do it, our shared instinctive reaction to trying to restart a stalled car.

I ask what time we are expected. I think I know the answer but ask anyway. Karma Yangki doesn't disappoint me. She shrugs. The Bhutanese seldom work to a timetable.

After about half an hour of driving almost straight up the side of the mountain, Phuntsho Wangmo stops the car. From here we must go by foot. It is a pleasant but rocky walk with mud and steep inclines. We pass Kathryn around among us, sharing the load.

We walk along the face of the mountain, glimpsing, through the dappled leaves of the forest, the valley laid out below us. It is a spectacular sight. There are a few houses dotted along the way then suddenly there is a group of them, a dozen clinging to the mountain side. Mostly they are made from stone with slate roofs, uneven wooden fences and loads of rustic charm. We follow a dirt path that meanders between them and finally stop at a rickety wooden gate, about 2.5 metres high, held closed by a piece of wire looped over a nail. Behind it, standing with its four feet aggressively splayed, is a huge black dog with yellow eyes and a fierce bark. This is it. The home of the shaman.

We all hesitate at the sight of the dog. From her handbag Phuntsho Wangmo pulls out her 'remote' phone, one of the handsets Mal has hired for the film, and dials the shaman's number. It seems delightfully incongruous – both that her remote phone works in this wildly inaccessible spot and that this isolated little patch of houses perched on the side of a hill is connected by telephone at all. But there you go. Another day, another misconception.

Although it has taken us so much time and effort to get here, it is only a few kilometres as the crow flies from Thimphu.

The phone is engaged and while we wait, the dog gets bored. He stops his aggressive posturing and pads over to a warm patch of sun to lie down, but facing us so we know he is still interested.

After a few minutes, with the telephone still engaged, Karma Yangki unhooks the nail and nudges open the gate. The dog watches but makes no move to get up. 'He's fine,' she whispers. We follow her in, stepping very carefully. Slow and silent. No sudden movements. I clutch Kathryn tightly to me, expecting her to be scared. Lord knows, I am. But she seems blissfully unperturbed.

Karma Yangki sees the look on my face and reassures me: 'It's okay. Just don't show fear.' Uh-huh. That helps enormously.

Karma Yangki avoids the path to the front door (which would take us past the dog) and heads straight up the side of the house. She disappears through a curtain covering the open back door while the rest of us stand around looking as non-threatening as we can, smiling at the dog, who has followed us around to the side of the house but is keeping his distance.

Karma Yangki pops her head out through the curtain and beckons us inside. The room we enter has wooden walls and floors and is completely bare except for three low benches. We sit on these, facing each other.

'She's on the telephone to a member of the royal family,' Karma Yangki tells us.

So we wait. A nasty smell pervades the little room and we lay Kathryn on the bench to change her nappy. Then we wait some more. Finally a woman appears in the doorway. She is not at all what I expect. While the three sisters are all in *kira*s, she is wearing trousers and a baggy red windcheater, with her hair cut in a short sculptured bob. She could be any mum from the suburbs.

The shaman leads us through another sparsely furnished room and into her bedroom, where she takes up her position cross-legged on the bed, pulling a blanket over her lap and tucking it around her bare feet. We sit opposite her – Phuntsho Wangmo, Kathryn and I on a carpet-covered bench running beneath the window, while Karma Yangki and Karma Chokyi are on the floor.

There is much friendly chat and smiles between the shaman and Karma Yangki, and I don't need to speak the language to have an idea what they are saying. *How have you been? I'm fine thanks, except for the cold. Oh yes, wasn't last night a killer... How's Mani Dorji? He's well, working hard. How's your mother/sister/family?* Or something like it.

The two women are obviously well acquainted and the other two sisters remain quiet, listening politely, as the conversation moves backwards and forwards.

The chat lasts a few minutes and then the mood in the room subtly changes. Karma Yangki gestures to me and the shaman turns her attention my way. She smiles at Kathryn then fixes her huge black eyes on me. Any semblance to a suburban mum disappears. She seems shiny, like a sleek well-fed cat. A lynx. Her black eyes bore right into me as Karma Yangki talks. Every now and then the shaman nods or raises her eyebrows or asks something. I would love to know what they are saying but don't want to interrupt the flow. The language they are speaking is worlds away from English so it isn't like I can catch odd words and figure it out.

The shaman's mouth and gums are tinged with red spittle from the betel nut she constantly chews and she dabs at her mouth with a colourful scarf. She obviously spends a lot of time right here, sitting on the bed. From where she is, she can reach over to a small cassette player and a pile of tapes. The plastic covers show men in Bhutanese dress with exotic-looking instruments I don't recognise. A plastic soap container and toothbrush are next to one knee. Scattered around her are a couple of books, a silver goblet and oddly, three handbags.

She opens one of these and withdraws a small ornate pillbox, shiny black, like onyx, with a golden dragon carved on the surface. As she and Karma Yangki continue to talk, the shaman takes out a single die, which she holds in her hand, as if weighing it, and peers at the shiny surface inside the pillbox lid.

Karma Yangki asks me in English for the name of the book I am currently writing. I tell her. *The Wrong Door*. She repeats it, in English, and the shaman nods, still rolling the die around in her hand and peering into the lid of the pillbox.

She and Karma Yangki talk together. (How long does it take to say 'It will be a raging bestseller'? I wonder.)

Finally Karma Yangki turns to me and nods. 'It's okay,' she says.

I wait for more. Five minutes of chatting and nodding must have produced more than two words, but the shaman is talking again.

Phuntsho Wangmo leans close to me and explains some of what was said. 'There is a well-respected man who thinks highly of you. He will champion your books. You will always have enough money,' she whispers. 'It's all good.'

Karma Yangki and the shaman continue to talk backwards and forwards. I recognise the word 'Kathryn'. The way Karma Yangki pronounces it is lovely, like *Cut-Trin*. The shaman responds and suddenly all three sisters smile – at each other and at Kathryn. There is lots of nodding and sounds of agreement. Even Kathryn is smiling. She seems to be in on whatever it is that's going on.

Phuntsho Wangmo starts translating again: 'She says Kathryn has a strong connection with Bhutan. She will come back here again and again. And she will always be safe here. She has a protector.'

The women are all smiling. This is wonderful news.

Phuntsho Wangmo asks if I have any questions. Boy, do I. But we've been talking about me for more than half an hour already, so it must be Karma Chokyi's turn. I bite my tongue and shake my head.

I expect Karma Chokyi to speak up but Karma Yangki takes the lead. As she and the shaman discuss the blossoming love affair, Karma Chokyi is on tenterhooks, wide-eyed and alert. I recognise Dr Thinley's name. Whatever the shaman is saying causes Karma Chokyi to blush and lower her head. That has to be a good sign. But as the shaman continues, her smile starts to fade – not so promising. The shaman has plenty to say, and Phuntsho Wangmo and Karma Yangki ask many questions. At each one the shaman rolls the die in her hand and looks back into the pillbox. Sometimes she tosses the die into the box, then gently rolls it around in there. All the time she is talking.

Finally she stops. The room is silent while the sisters consider what she has said. I'm bursting to know what has gone on.

'Is it okay?' I whisper to Karma Chokyi. She nods but looks away.

Phuntsho Wangmo asks about the film. It will be a big success, says the shaman.

We say our farewells and her parting words are that Mal and I must bring Kathryn back to Bhutan. She will be happy here, she says, looking at Kathryn. The shaman walks with us out the back door, to the gate. The dog follows obediently behind her, not making any unfriendly noises.

As we make our way down the track, Phuntsho Wangmo talks about different things the shaman has told her over the years about love affairs and business. She has complete confidence in everything she says.

It isn't until we get back into the car that I find out what was said about Karma Chokyi. The shaman said she and Dr Thinley could prosper together but it would not be good for the family. Now I understand the change of mood in the room. So it's the family or the boyfriend. An awful choice. But if this is bad news it doesn't show. The sisters chat cheerfully all the way home.

※

Mal tries to ring every few days but communication from the new camp is fraught with difficulty. The system is solar-powered and the signal bounces off various hills from a duplex radio transmitter about an hour up the road, finally reaching camp through an aerial tied to a tree that tips out of alignment when the wind blows, which is often. On days with fog or clouds, it just doesn't work.

Desperate to receive emails from the editors in Australia, Mal visited a local family forty-five minutes' drive away, who kindly poked their telephone, with its primitive wiring, through a window in their kitchen for him to use.

Unfortunately the line was so bad that after many minutes of juggling his laptop on his knee while curious children gathered around, he had to admit defeat. He tells me all this over an echoing phoneline that makes it sound like he is in a wind tunnel, while I sit warm and comfortable in the Taba home, nodding to the maids that yes, I would love more tea.

※

Along with two little dogs, the family has two ginger kittens. They are only a few months old and completely skittish. They chase each other everywhere – up and down the stairs, along curtain rails and all over the furniture. Often when I'm sitting up in bed working they will race in the open door and onto the bed, tumbling off onto the rug as they grapple with each other. Kathryn is completely captivated by them and squeals with delight when they stand still long enough for her to pat their fur.

The family bought them to help with the rat problem. There are lots of rats in the roof and I can hear them at night rustling and crying out. I grew up with possums in the roof so the sound doesn't worry me or keep me awake. They aren't particularly interested in coming into our room, so I'm not concerned for Kathryn. It is the shrine room next door that is the big drawcard.

Early each morning Karma Chokyi says prayers and makes offerings for the family. The bowls of rice and butter lamps, constantly kept fresh, are like a smorgasbord for the rats. Karma Chokyi believes that a big fat one lives in the room, hiding until she leaves. She has glimpsed him scurrying off when she opens the door.

One night one of the kittens earns her keep, cornering a huge rat in the bathroom. It is twice the kitten's size but she is fearless, turning it into her own bedtime snack. From that moment on, the kittens are divided. The cat who ate the rat is intensely proud of her victory and stalks around upstairs looking to repeat her moment of glory. The other kitten, not nearly so brave, refuses to go anywhere near the bathroom and isn't too fond of coming up the stairs. There are brief moments of mutual play but mostly they become the upstairs and downstairs cats.

※

Karma Yangki is worried that I am not seeing enough of Thimphu's sights and organises a driving tour of the capital. As well as Trashi Chhoe Dzong and the National Memorial Chorten, she wants to show me the Bhutanese Broadcasting Service's tower, high on the hill above the city. (I've seen enough TV transmitting towers in my time so I'm not really keen but don't want to be rude.)

It is a favourite parking spot for lovers and when we get there, I can see why. The view across the valley is superb. But it would be a shame if the lovers stayed in the car. What makes this place truly breathtaking is further up the hill, which means a steep walk.

While I huff and puff, Karma Yangki hoists Kathryn effortlessly into her arms and strides on ahead, her *kira* billowing about. Hundreds of tall prayer flags flap in the strong breeze. They are made from stiff cotton that is covered in prayers which the Bhutanese believe are carried to the heavens by the wind. Standing in the midst of them is like being surrounded by a vast orchard of tall, skinny trees. The sound of their flapping is so loud that Karma Yangki and I have to yell to each other to be heard. Even so, there is an extraordinary sense of peace and serenity. Each year on a particular date, lamas and monks come here to say prayers and make offerings to the local deities for the wellbeing of all who live in Thimphu. For the rest of the year it's a popular picnic spot.

On the other side of the hill is a cluster of small wooden houses and Karma Yangki leads me through a rickety gate. A stooped old lady opens the door, her lined and weather-beaten face breaking into a broad grin at the sight of us.

'This is Mani Dorji's mother,' explains Karma Yangki.

The tiny two-room house is immaculate – not a skerrick of dust or dirt to be seen. On the walls hang a hot water bottle and a calendar.

Karma Yangki's mother-in-law disappears to make us tea. After a few moments a young girl carries it in on a tray. She is concentrating very hard and takes small, careful steps so as not to spill anything.

The girl is about eight and lives here with the old lady. Her mother was struggling to bring her up on her own in a country village. Mani Dorji's mother took in the little girl and organised a job for the mother as a live-in cook with a family nearby.

The little girl lives here, going to school and helping around the house.

While we chat, the girl stands partly hidden behind the old lady, overcome with shyness. Every time I smile at her, she retreats a little bit further. It is only when we leave that I'm treated to a huge grin, revealing a row of beautiful even white teeth.

Next stop on our tour is an enormous warehouse on the edge of town where about a dozen women are sitting on the floor, weaving *kira*s on their backstrap looms. The owner comes to greet us and leads us into his office, which is stacked floor to ceiling with bolts of fabric. Hanging on every wall are beautiful *kira*s which the owner points to lovingly.

He is cheeky, flamboyant and wiggles his hips in an outrageously suggestive manner when he walks. He brings out some of his more expensive *kira*s for us to admire and talks about them with immense passion, discussing at length the colours and patterns.

The man is gay, no doubt about it. I suggest this to Karma Yangki, curious to see her reaction. She doesn't seem particularly shocked, just doesn't know what I am talking about. Bhutan doesn't have gay men, she says.

Maybe not, but I have no doubt that man would be perfectly at home on Sydney's Oxford Street.

8

Lady Muck

The sisters anticipate anything I might desire and have the maids cater to it. They are all so kind that it's driving me nuts. I'm not used to having servants, and it makes me feel guilty. As they clear away my plates and bring yet more tea I can't throw the feeling that my grandmother might appear at any time and tell me off for lying around like Lady Muck. An unforgivable sin when I was growing up.

So I try to help, taking my own dishes down to the kitchen after a meal. It doesn't work. Either I get shooed away by a giggling maid before I even make it down the stairs or the plates are whisked off me at the kitchen doorway by one of the sisters, her face friendly but disapproving.

I can't tell if they are being polite or actually would rather I didn't go into their kitchen. Heaven knows, it isn't my room of choice and I strive to spend as little time in my own as possible. But every time they do something for me I hear echoes of my grandmother's accusing voice.

I decide that I'm committing a cultural faux pas with my inisistence on appearing in their kitchen and instead sit back, letting it all happen around me. After a meal I leave the dishes on the table and go back to work.

When I tell Mal about it on his next visit he is horrified and says I have to persevere. The sisters are just being polite and I mustn't make the mistake of falling into an 'upstairs downstairs' kind of arrangement. So often westerners mis-understand Bhutanese generosity – they might offer you their last mouthful or the *gho* off their back but that doesn't mean you should take it, he says. Even if the sisters continue to chase me out of the kitchen, the gesture will be appreciated.

Mal should know. For the past decade he has enjoyed the hospitality of Rinpoche's people all over the world and is used to being a guest in Asian homes. I watch partly envious and partly horrified at how he slips in and out of life at Taba.

When he is here he takes over the formal lounge room, commandeers the telephone for film business and merrily leaves his washing out on the landing for the maids. It is clear he feels perfectly at home. I, on the other hand, stay out of the formal lounge room except when the other sisters are with me, try to do my own washing and haven't quite managed to throw the feeling that I am on my best behaviour.

He tries to explain the subtleties of Asian hospitality with what he calls his two-week rule. It's always a dynamic, he stresses, but loosely speaking, if you are staying for less than two weeks then expect to be treated like a special, honoured guest. Be grateful and courteous but accepting of it all. Any longer and it's up to you to start to become part of the household.

He explains that the Bhutanese would find it funny that I would try to do the maids' job – clearing away dishes – when that is what they are paid to do. The same with my washing. Let the maids do their jobs. I must find other ways to help. It's all about attitude, he says, leaving me more confused than ever. Relax and become part of the family, but don't for a minute stop trying to help.

He sees the look of bewilderment on my face and tries to reassure me that any social faux pas I make will be forgiven on the basis that I am a foreigner. But, he adds helpfully, if it's real and lasting respect I'm after, it would be best if I don't lose it to start with.

And then he is gone again, back up the yak trail, the next set of rushes in his hot little hand and a truckload of crises to deal with, leaving me to tiptoe around these wonderfully generous people, terrified lest secretly they think I'm behaving like Lady Muck.

❋

Eventually I do relax. It's impossible not to, surrounded by such harmony and happiness. The paper-thin walls echo with laughter and the sound of women calling out 'ana, ana', which is their word for 'sister'.

Each of them has a different way of relating to Kathryn, and she responds accordingly. She waves back to Karma Yangki, claps with Karma Chokyi, opens her mouth and eyes wide when she sees Renee and Phuntsho Wangmo, and with Wesel Wangmo, she makes a bird-like coo.

Teaching her to crawl has become a family exercise and everybody is in on it. Her training ground is, naturally, the most popular spot in the house – that much-trafficked patch of floor beside Karma Yangki's bed. This is where Wesel Wangmo and Karma Chokyi watch TV; where Mani Dorji repairs his suitcase on a leisurely Sunday; and where Karma Yangki threads her wool. It's also where cousins and friends sit to enjoy a chat, a bowl of cornflakes and sweetened tea.

In the midst of whatever is going on is Kathryn, face down balancing on her stomach as she tries to co-ordinate her arms and legs. Her adopted Bhutanese family cheer her on, getting down on all fours to show her how.

One afternoon I wander down to find Kathryn and Wesel Wangmo, Karma Chokyi and a couple of cousins sitting in a large circle. While Renee and Madonna are trying on the big girls' jewellery, the sisters have dyed Kathryn's scalp with henna. She is sitting in the middle of the circle, wearing rows of necklaces and a huge smile. She looks gorgeous and exotic, and I wonder how the hell they managed it. This baby that screams the house down whenever we wash her hair, has been given a henna rinse, without a whimper reaching me upstairs. Amazing!

Phuntsho Wangmo tells me the family feel a very strong connection with Kathryn, unlike anything they have felt for a baby outside their own immediate circle. And the feeling is obviously mutual. Seeing how they all relate is really quite special.

☀

Karma Yangki invites me to the best spa and beauty 'saloon' in Thimphu and I can't think of a better way to spend an afternoon.

Karma Yangki isn't as confident about her English as her younger sisters so when we arrive she doesn't explain much – just hands me a towel and leads me down the corridor to a door marked 'Ladies'. Inside is a toilet, a washbasin with mirror, two showers and a heavy glass door so covered in steam that we can't see through it.

Every surface, including the cold floor, is awash with icy water so we hop from foot to foot while juggling our shoes and clothes, and strip naked. Karma Yangki wipes a corner of the vanity dry and we put our belongings in a pile. A quick shower then it's through the heavy glass door. The steam room is a cubicle with a bench big enough for two. It is wonderfully, gloriously hot and smells of lemon grass. Within seconds I'm the warmest I've been since arriving. It's heaven . . . for an instant . . . then it's too hot. I last an embarrassingly short amount of time while Karma Yangki sits and sweats, somehow looking demure even as the perspiration pours off her.

We move from the steam room to the changing room and

back again, enjoying the heat then cooling off. When we've had enough, we find that two other women have arrived and we have to wait our turn for the showers.

We stand on the cold floor, dressed only in our towels, and it doesn't take long before we cool right down. The water is icy cold under our bare feet. I react by putting on my shoes. Karma Yangki reacts in a way that is so Bhutanese and so Karma Yangki that I feel completely humbled. In the time it takes me to think how annoying it is, she checks behind the toilet door and finds a mop. Without fuss or comment she cleans away all the water. In a matter of minutes the room is more comfortable for me, the two women in the showers and anyone else who might follow.

Surely it is this generosity of spirit and basic kindness that makes the culture so harmonious.

Then it's down the corridor for a bit of a touch-up. Karma Yangki leads me to the 'saloon', which is the size of a small bathroom with two chairs side by side in front of a long mirrored counter. A couple of posters for make-up products are taped to the wall. A woman is already having her eyebrows plucked and Karma Yangki takes a seat beside her. I watch from the only available spot, an old-fashioned barber's chair, which takes up most of the floor space. It's where the men come for a close shave with a cut-throat razor.

It doesn't matter that the seat springs have gone because I don't stay there long, moving closer to try to work out what they are doing to Karma Yangki and the other woman. The two beauty therapists work in perfect symmetry, taking a long piece of cotton thread and moving it with their fingers in a scissor motion across their clients' eyebrows. Somehow, each time, they remove a single hair.

It's like watching someone do a complicated chopstick manoeuvre, very quickly, only without the chopsticks. And all the while the four women are chatting and laughing, catching up on the latest gossip of Thimphu, like middle-class ladies in beauty parlours all over the world.

Thimphu's first 'saloon' opened in the 1990s but now there are about twenty of them, offering all manner of beauty treatments.

After ten minutes or so they are finished and Karma Yangki asks what I think of her newly neatened eyebrows. They are beautifully arched but the skin around them looks pink and painful, as if someone has just pinched her very hard.

'They look sore,' I say. 'Did it hurt?'

'Yes,' she replies.

We both nod. Of course it hurts. Stupid question. Plucking hairs from your eyebrows always hurts, whether it's with hot wax, tweezers or cotton thread and a nifty wrist action.

'But they look better, yes?' she adds with a grin.

Can't argue with that. Beauty may be only skin deep but it would seem that the pursuit of it is universal. I feel right at home.

✳

Brothers Mani Dorji and Tenzin Wangdi take off for a few days to Phuntsoling, the border town eight hours' drive away where the presses are situated.

The family company, KMT, is the country's largest privately owned press. It started out twenty-five years ago printing Buddhist texts from wooden blocks for monasteries. Today it produces everything from colour brochures and writing pads to textbooks, and has interests in trading, stationery, hardware, electricals and electronics.

Tenzin Wangdi recently represented the brothers in Geneva, accepting an international award for business excellence. As strange as it may seem, this small company of a hundred employees, quietly going about its business in a small town on the edge of this little-known country, was recognised for an award previously won elsewhere in the world by oil companies, space stations, drug companies, shipping lines and airlines. This family is going places. They have lots of plans for future projects, including launching their own newspaper. Where will their business be in ten years, I wonder.

While the brothers are away, their wives, Phuntsho Wangmo and Karma Yangki, join me one evening in the lounge room.

Over dinner on our laps, Phuntsho Wangmo asks the plot of the book I'm working on. A dog-eared copy of my second book, *The Affair*, has been doing the rounds of the family since I loaned it to Karma Chokyi a few days after arriving. I keep seeing it on a table or by a bed in different rooms around the house. I have no idea what they make of it. There is no such thing as a fiction writer in Bhutan. The books published here are about Bhutanese heroes and history, or great Buddhist masters.

I explain that the new one I am working on is called *The Wrong Door* and begins when a woman goes to the wrong funeral service. Her appearance is the catalyst for the story that unfolds.

Phuntsho Wangmo laughs with delighted recognition. It happens all the time in Bhutan, she tells me. They hold many cremations at the same spot, on the same auspicious date, and it is Bhutanese custom to leave money for the family. Often, she says, you turn up to the service, give your money, then realise you don't recognise anyone. You're at the wrong service. But you can't exactly ask for your money back. It is really embarrassing to then find the right service and not have any money left for the family. She laughs and laughs. 'I like your plot,' she says. 'Very Bhutanese.'

They tell me the story of a woman in Thimphu who is supposed to have murdered her lover's wife. According to local gossip, she lured the unsuspecting wife to a secluded spot then ran her off the road. She is now living happily with the husband.

Murder is not entirely new to Bhutan but it is rare. Even so, this kind of premeditated crime is both shocking and un-thinkable. The sisters don't know the people involved but are horrified at the whole sorry saga. (The way they see it, crime doesn't just happen to other people, it happens in other countries. Like America. Or India. Or that whole alien world brought to them via cable TV.)

The murder comes just as Bhutan is losing its innocence in other ways. The nation is still reeling from the shock of its first major financial scandal, a group of Thimphu businessmen caught smuggling gold into the country.

Whether or not crime is increasing, or just the reporting of it, is a constant source of discussion in homes and shops, and in the lively letters page of the national newspaper, *The Kuensel*, where readers worry about the influence that TV and the internet might be having on their children.

It's not that crime is running rampant on the streets. Far from it. But change is happening at breakneck speed and the people are trying to keep up.

Things I take for granted – and which occurred slowly, over hundreds of years, in other countries – have arrived here in a bewilderingly short space of time. Until the 1960s the Bhutanese lived fruitful and happy lives without money, roads, electricity, telephones, schools, hospitals, a postal service or any visitors from outside. Infant mortality rates were high and life expectancy low (in 1960 life expectancy was just thirty-five years; in 2002 it is sixty-six) but they enjoyed their simple life, travelling everywhere by foot, participating in their unique folk festivals and remaining happily unconnected from the technological changes sweeping the rest of the world.

❉

For his coronation in 1974, Dragon King Jigme Singye Wangchuck invited foreign visitors and the country's first hotel was built to accommodate them. The world was given a rare glimpse into this elusive little kingdom with its handsome people in their colourful clothes and strange customs.

Australia presented the Royal Government with a fleet of Ford Falcons. Before their arrival only a handful of Indian cars had travelled on the kingdom's first section of newly built bitumen road. One senior Bhutanese bureaucrat who was present for the grand occasion remembers the Falcons fondly. He said a new Rolls-Royce ferried the Indian president to proceedings while the Ford Falcons followed in a majestic processional line, each one carrying a dignitary or an ambassador. The Falcons lasted for years. Mal remembers being driven in one when he first visited the country in the early '90s. It had been repaired using bits and pieces from all the others.

Soon after the coronation, which revealed Bhutan to the world, the first paying tourists arrived. Until then, the handful of people that had been allowed into the country were personal guests of the royal family. The pioneer tourists were a group of trekkers led by Lars Eric Lindblad, founder of Lindblad Travel in the USA and known as the great grand-daddy of group tours. His group was given limited permits to visit designated parts of eastern Bhutan. They discovered unspoiled wilderness, pristine air and centuries-old monasteries clinging precariously to near-vertical hills. Its beauty and character was unlike anywhere else in the Himalayas.

In 1991 tourism was privatised by the Royal Government and these days there are over ninety tour operators. Tourists need permits to travel through different parts of the country, and some areas are out of bounds altogether – in the east of Bhutan, close to the borders of China and India.

Where other countries embrace the tourist dollar, this is the last thing to interest the Bhutanese. They have had a good look over their borders at the devastating and irreversible impact tourism can have on the local environment, culture and identity of the people. The King knew Bhutan couldn't remain an isolated medieval country forever and it was time to let the world in – but ever mindful of how to manage the influence from outside, he wanted to ensure it was done slowly and gently.

In keeping with his policy of Gross National Happiness, he decreed that tourism must be environmentally and ecologically sensitive, socially acceptable as well as economically viable. One way to achieve this would be to make it low volume and high value, charging a limited number of people US$250 per person per night.

It seems to be working – attracting the sort of tourists who won't upset the status quo. The people who come tend to be older, travelling in organised groups and they stay just a week or so. There are some newly opened clubs and bars in Thimphu but they aren't filled with backpacking westerners, rather the growing Bhutanese middle-class. The dance floors are full of young Bhutanese swivelling their hips, some dressed in the latest western-style clothes, others trying to groove to the music in a slim-fitting *kira*.

Also to commemorate the Dragon King's coronation, Bhutan created its own currency, the ngultrim, which is tied to the Indian rupee in value.

Twenty-five years later, at the King's Silver Jubilee in 1999, he further opened the doors to outside with the announcement of the arrival of TV and the internet. In the space of just one generation, the country has moved from a feudal society to one that is beginning to embrace the twenty-first century.

My newly adopted family at Taba perfectly encompasses the old and the new that is Bhutan. The sisters grew up in a village but live a thoroughly modern life in the country's capital.

Elder sister Karma Yangki and husband Mani Dorji were born in the '60s, just as education became available. They were teenagers in the '70s when outsiders first entered the country and cars started to appear on the newly built roads. And now they are parents and businesspeople, as the country cautiously takes its place in the world.

Second sister Phuntsho Wangmo, in her early thirties, spent a few years working in hotel management in Austria. She has seen the world and keeps in contact with the European friends she made. But, like most of the Bhutanese who work or study overseas, she came home. Though the career opportunities are far more limited and she was overqualified for the hospitality jobs she was offered back in Thimphu, there was never any question of her making her life elsewhere. What the rest of the world has to offer just doesn't compare with what she has in Bhutan.

When the family decided to expand the printing company and buy a franchise for the popular Indian card shop Archies, her management experience made her the obvious choice to run the business.

For some reason Archies, the old American comic strip, is enormously popular in India and though completely unrelated, so is the card shop. The Indians love to send sentimental cards at every opportunity. Opening an Archies shop in Thimphu, selling cards along with photographs of Buddhist icons and assorted stationery items, was an inspired business decision and overnight the shop was a huge success. Everyone in Thimphu knew Archies and it became a landmark in the town. The bus stop opposite was labelled 'The bus stop near Archies'. Thimphu had never seen anything like it.

Unfortunately for Phuntsho, while she was launching Archies, her new husband Tenzin was best qualified to run the day-to-day operations of the family printing press in Phunt-soling, eight hours away. It meant spending the start of their marriage either apart or commuting between the two cities as they pursued their different careers.

※

In many ways the Bhutanese are thoroughly modern, and sexism doesn't work quite the same way as it does elsewhere. Though women may be in charge of the domestic duties and are not yet filling the inner sanctum of Cabinet, they are, quite literally, everywhere else – working as doctors, engineers, teachers, running farms, owning businesses and holding senior positions throughout the government. They are well represented in district-level decision-making and treated equally in education and wages. In 2000, more than forty-six per cent of the primary school enrolments were girls.

When it comes to owning real estate, surely Bhutanese women lead the world. In rural areas sixty per cent of land is registered to women. It's known as 'customary right of inheritance by daughters', a system that has arisen because it is believed that women need economic security to be able to take care of their parents and children.

Sexism does exist. The royal family is patriarchal, passing the title from father to son, and the monastic culture is male-oriented. While there are more monks than soldiers, the nuns are a bit thin on the ground.

The story of Bhutan's first woman soldier is a delightful example of how the women just go about things. In 1962, twenty-three-year-old Tshering Bidha was one of thousands who volunteered for military service. Her husband was joining up and she thought, why not? She had a baby daughter so brought her mother along to babysit. During breaks in guerrilla-warfare training, her mother would bring the baby to her for breastfeeding. Tshering not only passed her training, she topped the school, beating her husband.

She gleefully recounted to *The Kuensel* newspaper how, as a senior officer, she would punish him for teasing other women soldiers by making him carry a thirty-kilo sand bag for an hour. She is now sixty-three, retired and a sweet, wrinkly grandmother, whose reminiscences also include anecdotes from her years as a crack soldier.

※

The amazing success that Phuntsho Wangmo achieved with the Archies card shop was duly noted by other companies and soon rival shops started to spring up, including the international stationery giant Hallmark. It was time for the family to get out. Phuntsho Wangmo went to Delhi and dissolved the partnership with Archies head office and then joined her husband in Phuntsoling. They bought two new apartments and knocked out a wall to create one large, comfortable home with all the modern conveniences.

Phuntsoling is far more cosmopolitan than Thimphu and yet toned down compared to the complete chaos of Indian cities. Its climate is more hot Indian plains than the cool of the Himalayan valleys. It is humid, dusty, noisy and pretty funky.

Phuntsho Wangmo prefers the grace and ease of life in Thimphu but was happy at last to be under the same roof with her husband and baby daughter Renee. Unfortunately it didn't last long.

The family re-thought what to do with its shops and created a new blended business. Cards and stationery sell in the shop that used to be Archies, while next door is a new hardware and electrical store, which also sells art supplies. The two shops take up nearly a whole block.

Again Phuntsho Wangmo was the obvious choice to start the hardware business but Tenzin was still needed in Phuntsoling to run the production side of the printing. So the commuting began again.

As Phuntsho Wangmo was still breastfeeding, the family converted two storerooms above the shop for her to be able to bring Renee to work. When they aren't living at Taba, or their real home in Phuntsoling, this is where they live – at the top of steep steps that are little more than a ladder, in two simply furnished rooms. Every morning Phuntsho Wangmo emerges down those steps looking elegant in a beautiful *kira*, her hair immaculate in its short, bouncy bob, and on her feet wedge shoes that I swear must be six inches high. I don't know how she can walk in them, much less make it up and down those steps. 'All Bhutanese women want to be taller,' she says with a smile and a shrug.

There is a warren of rooms behind the two shopfronts and somewhere in there Mani Dorji has his office, overseeing all the various businesses. Phuntsho Wangmo has two rooms, which double as her office for the hardware shop and the headquarters for Prayer Flag Pictures (which she also runs). She is a relaxed, efficient dynamo, juggling motherhood and the demands of her career with complete ease. She is lucky to have the support of her extended family, maids and her husband. Not all middle-class Bhutanese husbands are so accommodating, preferring to see themselves as the sole bread-winners. A wife leading a life of leisure is a new phenomenon that is emerging along with the growing affluence.

Behind the shops and all the offices are various outhouses, including a kitchen. Each day lunch is prepared by the maid, then spread out buffet style for anybody who happens to be there.

It was from these shops that sisters Phuntsho Wangmo and Karma Yangki did the initial casting for Rinpoche's film. With just an early draft of the script to work from, they would watch from behind a one-way mirror at the back of the shop, as people browsed through the cards. If someone looked promising they would sidle up for a bit of a chat and an informal interview.

It is typical of the way this family smoothly integrates everything into their lives. When Rinpoche needed somewhere to hold the auditions, they just added to the house at Taba, extending across the roof to create the formal lounge room. And when one of the producers wanted to bring his partner and child along, they happily volunteered their home. Whatever circumstances arise, they work with them. No angst. No dramas. Perhaps Nike had them in mind with their slogan 'Just Do It'.

9

Yak, Yak, Yak

In town I find a book of Bhutanese proverbs, written in English.

'The Mithun bull will pass his dung on either side of the road.' (I'm thinking, men sowing their wild oats?)

'Alcohol goes down, chat comes up.'

'Without wealth you are separated from your fellow beings but without teeth you are separated from food.' (Some things are much more important than money?)

But the one that really takes my fancy is: 'Every game has a nose, every nose smells a fart.' I ask Karma Chokyi what it means but she has no idea. She says she'll ask a boy at school who endlessly quotes obscure proverbs to her. I'm pleased and looking forward to dropping it into conversation at home when it's appropriate. ('As they say in Bhutan . . .')

❋

While Kathryn and I enjoy life with our new family, Mal comes and goes, bringing unprocessed film to send to Bangkok or picking up rushes to take back to an eager director and crew.

This week when Mal rings, he sounds so different that at first I don't recognise the voice. It's the giggling that throws me. He is by nature a pretty cheery kind of guy, even laughing in his sleep. But not like this. Not *giggling* down the phone at me.

He says he will be here after 11 but not after 12. For some reason he finds that enormously amusing, and he's off again.

It turns out he has been suffering a toothache for a few days and, after soldiering on, finally succumbed to some hefty pain-killers from the American location secretary, Noa Jones. He is completely gaga.

Tonight he is returning to Thimphu, along with all the crew, who are here for two days of R&R. It is the King's birthday and Bhutan is throwing a party.

Juggling the schedule around the needs of the different nationalities is a constant challenge. Indians need a couple of days off for a religious holiday, the Bhutanese need different days for their religious and national celebrations, the Nepalese drivers have their own festivals, while the western crew members require one day off in every seven, though not necessarily for religious pursuit. In between, they try to shoot a movie.

All the crew are exhausted and in dire need of this weekend off. If the first location camp in Paro Valley had seemed basic, compared to the latest one it was a health spa. If only they had realised how good they'd had it.

Chendebji camp, their current home away from home, is perched by a river at the bottom of a valley where the Queen Mother grazes her yaks. Accommodation is a bunch of bamboo and plastic huts, inside a barbed-wire fence meant to keep out the animals – not just yaks but wild panthers and the Himalayan black bears that howl through the night. The Hollywood cinematographer has dubbed it 'Changi', after the prisoner-of-war camp in Singapore, and wanders around whistling the theme from the old classic *The Bridge on the River Kwai*.

The topography of the area means an icy wind rushes up the river and across the valley, chilling everything in its path. Everyone is hating the cold, westerners and Bhutanese alike. But the lighting designer, Ray Peschke, is suffering the most. He is in agony. Ray spends his life commuting between sunny Los Angeles, for work, and even sunnier Costa Rica, where he lives with his wife and daughter. Chendebji is his idea of a frozen hell. Each day he moves a little more slowly. To thaw him out an electric bar heater is bought in Thimphu and sent up by car, along with a load of rushes and supplies.

Life isn't all grim at Chendebji camp. To offset some of the hardships two luxurious outdoor Bhutanese baths have been built. They are wooden with a compartment at one end where stones are added straight from the fire. As each stone is dropped in, it spits and sends up clouds of steam. Bathers stay in it as long as they can handle the temperature, which, unlike western-style baths, increases as the stones release more and more heat. The Bhutanese say half an hour in one of those keeps them warm for a week. The accommodation department fires up the baths every evening and there is a steady procession through them until late into the night.

The water doesn't get changed and there is a protocol that goes with bathtime. It's Rinpoches in first and a fight for who gets to go next, picking up any stray blessings that may be floating in the bathwater. Then it's everybody else, according to mob rule. The idea is to wash thoroughly with soap before entering the water but it doesn't always happen. No-one seems terribly concerned. When it's this cold, why quibble.

But the absolute highlight of being on location is the food. Napoleon said an army marches on its stomach and so, to keep up morale, Mal has made food the highest priority.

There are twenty-five people in the catering department, working out of two kitchens and providing traditional Bhutanese, Indian and continental food. They built their own tandoori oven and serve the food buffet style with the vast selection of dishes – at least a dozen – beautifully presented in huge elegant, bain marie serving dishes that would be perfectly at home in an exclusive hotel.

Every night, under the stars in the pristine wilds of Bhutan – warmed by an outdoor bonfire while being serenaded by grass-munching yaks and the sound of rushing water from the nearby river – the 108 members of the cast and crew sit down to a gourmet feast. Meals are a social and culinary event that are longed for and lingered over.

One of the head chefs is a gentle, smiling Tibetan man who lives in Manali, in northern India. Yeshe Lama usually works as a chef on forty-five-day treks and specialises in creating gourmet continental food for rich tourists from what can be carried on the back of a horse. His two great loves are cooking and walking and he says he will be happy to forgo his return ticket so he can walk home to Manali, almost the entire length of the Himalayas.

Mal leaves Chendebji camp early in the afternoon and it is after midnight by the time he arrives at Taba. The painkillers have worn off and he looks grey. The evening chill and the high mountain passes on the trip have exacerbated his toothache. But nothing can daunt his enthusiasm for the thoughtful gift he has brought me – a yak-tail rug. Yaks are hardy creatures, used to surviving in the most inhospitable of terrains, so their fur is pretty tough. The hair on their tails is even more so. This rug is like steel wool – dark grey and hurts to touch. Mal thinks it will be perfect for the hallway of our harbourside apartment. I try to imagine walking barefoot across steel wool to get to the fridge each morning. Not good.

All the crew are sporting new yak accoutrements. As the weather turns colder the yaks come down from the mountains and in the past week there were quite a few around the pass where the crew was filming. One enterprising herdsman followed the crew back to camp and brought a few bags along to sell. They were snapped up in an instant. The next day the man returned, lugging with him his entire 'range'. He had more bags, blankets and a couple of things made from the tail of the yak, including a rug. Again he sold the lot. Mal bought yak-hair bags as gifts from the production company to every foreign member of the crew and, bless him, the yak-tail rug for me.

We wake to the smell of a yak in the bedroom. It's discernible even above Kathryn's morning nappy and, despite the nausea it inspires, secretly I'm pleased. There's no way Australian customs will let us bring this rug into the country.

※

Kathryn is delighted to see Mal's face peer over her cot in the morning. He brings her back to bed and a maid appears with hot tea. We really could get used to this.

The film dramas follow Mal and he doesn't make it through breakfast before the phone calls start. I'm no movie-making expert but I can't imagine that the problems that crop up for this production company would occur often in Hollywood.

For the past week filming has been disrupted by demons. Evil spirits that the Bhutanese say are irritated by the positive energy of Rinpoche. This comes after some worrying calls from the anxious editors in Sydney, who say mysterious blue spots have started to appear on the film. Above the heads of two actors appear oddly shaped haloes. The camera people check all their equipment and can offer no explanation. It's just one of those things, they shrug. It's bad spirits, say the Bhutanese.

Between phone calls, Mal fills me in on what has happened over the past week. They had been shooting scenes in a cave by the side of the road at a particularly beautiful spot, but it felt eerie. Everyone was aware of it. There was trouble on the set, with disagreements among the crew and lots of niggly little things going wrong.

The troubles came to a climax with an accident to the main camera. According to people there at the time, no-one bumped it, there was no gust of wind and no traffic on the road nearby to cause vibrations. The camera was standing by itself, secure on a tripod, when it just fell over on the spot.

The Bhutanese blame the Demoness, a particularly nasty spirit, believed to live opposite the site where they were filming. They say she was unsettled by the presence of Rinpoche and was fighting his positive energy.

The camera that fell over started making unhealthy noises. It's a very sophisticated Aaton XTP Prod, brought over from Hollywood by cinematographer Alan Kozlowski. The only way to know how badly it has been damaged is to shoot some film, have it processed and look at the results. That means getting a test reel onto a Druk Air flight to Bangkok, then to the processing lab, as quickly as possible.

Somehow, in the peculiarly Bhutanese way of doing things, this is achieved. Because the country is so small, everyone is connected, and all business is done by tapping into the network of family. Someone on the crew has a sister who is married to someone else's cousin who works at the airport and who is married to . . .

With James Bond precision, the test reel is driven for five hours to be handed to a Druk Air pilot before dawn on a stretch of road outside Thimphu. He carries it in his hand luggage, presenting it at Bangkok Airport to an official from the Bhutanese Embassy. She then drives it to the lab.

Mal, his face still aching from his bad tooth, takes call after call keeping him up to date with the movements of that little film canister. It is unprocessed film and the last thing they need is for a security person to insist on opening it – a definite possibility in the current terrorist-alert state of the world.

If the results show that the main camera is damaged, they will need to get a new one sent over from America, which will take time and mean rescheduling scenes around what can be shot on the second camera. It is a scary scenario for everybody. As I am absorbing the ramifications, Mal, despite his tooth pain, seems remarkably calm. In fact he's *enjoying* himself. He laughs at my bewilderment. No, he hasn't taken any more

hefty painkillers, he assures me. He just has no doubt everything will turn out okay.

Before Mal started ringing around Bhutan to organise the
safe passage of the test reel, Rinpoche had telephoned Orgyen
Tobgyal Rinpoche, the high Tibetan lama who lives in India
and performed all the *mos* (divinations) for the film. Orgyen
Tobgyal picked up the phone and without preamble, cheerfully
asked what Rinpoche was doing surrounded by so many
demons.

His *mo* said that the camera hadn't been damaged in the fall
but that the foreign crew would be worried and want to get it
tested anyway, so let them, and the results will show it is fine.
Knowing the outcome has taken the pressure off and Mal is
having a lovely time fielding calls from anxious crew members,
wanting to know if the lab has called with the test results.

At lunchtime the Bangkok lab finally does call. The test
footage is all good. No discernible damage. Word quickly
spreads throughout the crew and with the relief comes much
laughter and raising of eyebrows. Even the most sceptical are
starting to think there may be something in this *mo* stuff.

The camera incident also marks a turning point. During
pre-production Orgyen Tobgyal had warned that there would
be plenty of hiccups but one major obstacle. Unfortunately he
was unable to predict what it was. Rinpoche had passed this on
to Mal, who had been wondering, every time something went
wrong, if this was 'it'.

Orgyen Tobgyal confirmed it was. The big one was out of
the way. Phew. He could relax.

※

Meanwhile, back at the haunted pass, the local villagers are
doing just that. Relaxing. Their mood is upbeat and happy.
The site where the crew has been filming has been substantially
changed and they are enjoying the benefits.

The cave used in the scene is part of a small quarry by the

side of the highway between the towns of Chendebji and Rukabji. Rinpoche had a particular vision in mind for the scene that required the art department – Ugyen Wangchuk and his assistant, also called Ugyen Wangchuk, and Rinpoche's childhood friend, the monk artist Sonam Choepel – to paint on the side of a rock a three-metre-high head of Guru Rinpoche, the most important figure in Vajrayana Buddhism. Also known as the second Buddha, he brought Buddhism from India to Bhutan and Tibet in the eighth century.

Guru Rinpoche is credited with having had miraculous powers, such as the ability to subdue demons and make prophecies, including that in the modern age Buddhism would spread to the west: 'When the iron bird flies and horses run on wheels, the Tibetan people will be scattered like ants across the world and the Dharma will come to the land of the redman.'

No-one sought permission before painting this huge face on a rock in brightly coloured indelible paint, even though it is on Bhutan's busiest road, the Lateral Highway, and is guaranteed to stop cars in their tracks. Also, the painting will render the quarry unusable – no Bhutanese would dream of digging into an image of Guru Rinpoche. But they aren't big on rules in Bhutan and the locals are thrilled by the painting. Religious art is a tradition and apart from being incredibly beautiful, the painting of Guru Rinpoche's face is a lasting reminder to the Demoness of the valley to behave herself.

At Rinpoche's instruction the two Ugyen Wangchuks also paint a *stupa* (like a shrine), a protector lion and a Buddhist teaching, known as the eight worldly dharmas, in English on a huge rock by the side of the road.

May all sentient beings be free from wanting to be praised, not wanting to be criticized, wanting to be happy, not wanting to be unhappy, wanting to gain, not wanting to lose, wanting to be famous, not wanting to be ignored.
Thus prayed at the occasion of filming in Bhutan.

Each member of the crew then signs their name on the bottom of the rock.

Almost before the paint has dried, the site becomes a tourist attraction. The locals are indebted to Rinpoche, and not just because the rest of Bhutan is suddenly making its way to their door. They say that by filming and performing *puja*s, Rinpoche has subdued the legendary Demoness. This is an unexpected blessing. All their lives they have lived in the shadow of her negative energy and at last they feel they can sleep easy.

✳

The 'major obstacle' may be out of the way, and the Demoness of the valley sorted out, but niggling problems and bad spirits continue to follow the crew around. The second camera takes a tumble in another mysterious, unexplainable accident.

This camera, a lightweight Aaton A-Minima, is used for aerial shots. The grips and camera department spend hours securing cable between two farmhouses, six metres above the ground. They test it twelve times for tension and try it out with weights much heavier than the camera. It is a relatively simple procedure that the highly experienced key grip Tom Lembcke, a stalwart of Hollywood films, must have done a hundred times before.

Tom, along with the directory of photography, the first assistant camera person, the technical co-ordinator and two Bhutanese assistants, is perched on the third floor of one house watching as the camera is sent down the cable. It makes it to the middle and is on its way back when there's a strange cracking noise. The twenty-by-twenty centimetre beam that is supporting the camera snaps, as they later say, 'like a brittle chicken bone'.

Everyone watching is aghast. How could it have happened? It makes no sense. This time the camera *is* damaged. The remote-control head no longer works, the body is scratched and it makes suspicious grinding noises as the film is wound through. It will have to go back to France to be repaired.

Rinpoche is not too concerned. It is only the small 'second' camera, and he was in two minds about using the aerial shot anyway. But cinematographer Alan Kozlowski is very concerned. The A-Minima is a much-valued piece of equipment and very expensive.

As producer, Mal must find out exactly what caused the accident and fill out an insurance form. He talks to everybody who was there. The foreigners aren't much help and give no insight into what happened – mostly because they still can't quite believe it did happen. They just keep shaking their heads and frowning. The Bhutanese, on the other hand, are happy to co-operate and give a full explanation. The farmhouse where the beam snapped is called 'the Black Roost' and known to be haunted. It was ghosts. No doubt about it, they say.

I try – and fail – to keep a straight face as Mal reads me what he has written in the form intended for the men in grey suits at the insurance company. Under 'cause' he has stated: 'Several witnesses have no doubt that spirit intervention played a role in the incident.'

In a few weeks, in an office somewhere in downtown Sydney, that form is going to land in someone's in-tray.

10

The Talk of Thimphu

When Mal is here, it is like being in the eye of a cyclone. After each visit, there is a momentary lull, then life returns to its comfortable routine with the family, the maids, Kathryn and myself.

The day starts around 6.30 with Kathryn's first cry. I bundle her back into bed for a feed and a cuddle. At about 7 am one of the maids brings tea; soon after Wesel Wangmo appears and takes Kathryn off for breakfast. Breakfast for me is at the dining table upstairs, surrounded by glass windows. First thing in the morning they're misty with condensation. After wiping a few panels I can eat breakfast and watch the morning fog slowly clear to reveal the mountains in all their majestic splendour.

This morning for breakfast it is Bhutanese tea with salt and butter, plus stewed potatoes and *japati*s (Indian-style fried flat bread), with *thukpa* (a hearty vegetable and pasta soup). The week I arrived I brought out my jar of Vegemite to have on toast but after its first appearance the maids took it downstairs and it hasn't reappeared since. Nor has toast. The breakfasts are far more elaborate than that. Occasionally, when I go into the kitchen to fill my thermos with boiling water, I see the Vegemite sitting on a very high shelf and look at it longingly. But I'm happy to eat whatever they put in front of me.

While I sip tea, in the driveway Mani Dorji's driver warms the engine and clears the ice from the windscreen. The car belongs to Mani Dorji and stays at Taba overnight in the driveway. The driver lives in Thimphu and catches an early bus here each morning. He is a short, dapper man with long argyle socks, pulled up to the knee around his muscly calves. It is so cold I can see the mist on his breath.

Students drift past the house alone and in groups of twos and threes on their way to school, which starts at 8.30. The older ones are peers of Karma Chokyi, dressed in *kiras* and *ghos* in the same orange and green checked fabric that she wears each day. The high school, built in 2001, is a few blocks along and I can see some of the grounds from my bedroom window. Also walking along are younger students, some only about six or seven, whose school is a few kilometres down the road. It seems like a long walk for such little people but they do it each weekday, trudging along with their books, laughing and chatting and chasing each other.

Foot traffic going the other way is less frequent. The occasional family group wanders by, carrying vegetables on their backs in large straw baskets, on their way to do business in Thimphu. The house opposite seems to be an unofficial bus stop because although there is no sign, throughout the day people congregate there, providing an ever-changing panorama to keep me entertained.

Taxis are frequent. They are like little kombi vans and pick up passengers all the way to the main street of Thimphu, dropping them off wherever they want to go. If the first one that comes by is full, another will be past shortly. The drivers seldom speak English, which means I have to use sign language and a map, though sometimes the other passengers help with explanations. A couple of times they've taken Kathryn on their knee for the trip.

While I enjoy breakfast, I see Karma Chokyi looking anxiously up the road for her cousin Karma Yogini to come by and walk with her. As she waits, she chats to Mani Dorji's driver. They both stamp their feet to keep warm and breathe out clouds of vapour.

Mani Dorji finally appears, handsome and businesslike in his *gho* and carrying a briefcase. As his car drives out, Karma Yogini walks in. She is the same age as Karma Chokyi and equally as beautiful. Her hair is also long and parted down the middle, but her face is broader and she has a cheeky smile, which she flashes often. One of the leads of Rinpoche's film, 'the hero' as they call him, is courting her. With that and Dr Thinley and what is happening at school, there is much for the two girls to giggle about.

✳

Romances between students at the high school are forbidden but, inevitably, a few flourish. Recently word of one made it to the ear of the headmaster. He asked at assembly for the guilty couple to come forward. No-one was more surprised than he was when five couples stood up. The shockwaves reverberated throughout the school, on to the parents, spilling out into the local community. It was a scandal of unthinkable proportions. The headmaster expelled the students, which Karma Chokyi thought was appropriate under the circumstances. The students could still sit for the end-of-year exams, only a few weeks away, just not under the banner of the school.

Karma Chokyi had her own brush with authority. After being late for a particular class the teacher told her to stand on the spot and do ten squats. She refused and came home, missing the class. Karma Chokyi is a diligent student so that seemed out of character. Over dinner that night she said she was upset by it. She hadn't meant to be rude or undermine the teacher, but, being shy, she couldn't bear being the focus of everybody's attention in such a way.

The next day she sought out the teacher to explain. She told him she was genuinely sorry about being late and would try to be on time in future. But, she added, squats were undignified. Doing them in the classroom would embarrass her. So even if she was late again, he shouldn't ask her to do them. So there. Go Karma Chokyi!

The teacher accepted her apology.

Education is freely available throughout Bhutan, after being introduced in the late 1950s. Before that it had only been available in the monasteries but these days education in secular schools from primary to tertiary level is available to most Bhutanese.

Dzongkha, the national language, is a compulsory subject although it isn't spoken in many of the students' homes, including here at Taba. Only one-fifth of the country speak it. Like most of eastern Bhutan, this family speaks Sharchop.

I discover this over dinner one night with Karma Chokyi. She explains how difficult she finds Dzongkha. It is her least favourite subject, even worse than mathematics. She sounds just like me. But as soon as I start thinking that way, feeling a sense of familiarity, someone will say something that rockets me back into the twilight zone.

Karma Chokyi explains that her native tongue has no written form. Sharchop is verbal only. There aren't any books or literature in the language. The sisters can't even write a shopping list or notes to each other using the words they speak every single day. It sounds so bizarre. These women, who are bright, funny and smart, with a wicked sense of humour, can't write down *anything* in their own language.

I ask how they leave notes for each other. Karma Chokyi looks confused.

'Why would we do that?'

'What if you take a telephone message for someone else in the family or just want to leave a note saying . . . I don't know

. . . you've borrowed your sister's jumper or won't be home till late because you've gone out with friends?'

'Oh,' says Karma Chokyi, suddenly understanding my concern. 'We would tell the maids. They're always here.'

Whenever Karma Chokyi or Wesel Wangmo needs to write something down they do it in English. But Karma Yangki's is not so good, nor is Mani Dorji's. However, they understand enough to read the English-language version of *The Kuensel*. It is also published in Dzongkha but they find that even harder.

In one of the family's shops in downtown Thimphu they sell cards, in English, that are very sentimental, much like you find in India. There are cards for every occasion, including some to wish students luck for exams. But this is a relatively modern phenomenon in Bhutan and the family isn't in the practice of giving each other cards for their birthdays or Christmas. They don't celebrate either occasion. The Buddhist equivalents are marked with prayers, not giving gifts or sending cards.

School classes are taught in English because originally there were so few Bhutanese teachers that they had to import them all. That's no longer the case and many graduates now choose a career in education, as teachers are such highly respected figures in the community.

While Karma Chokyi's dream is to be a fashion designer, in her more practical moments she considers becoming a teacher, perhaps of mathematics – even though she hates the subject. She figures it's just a bunch of formulas to learn by heart.

I ask her if there is a subject that she does enjoy and she says history. But there is so much to know and she fears a student might ask her a question she couldn't answer. She shakes her head. That would be too mortifying. Mathematics would be much safer.

One of the benefits of being taught in English is that many graduates have gone on to universities in America, Asia, Australia and Europe. They are encouraged to leave Bhutan to study and return with an international qualification. We look on the net for fashion schools in Australia. (Karma Chokyi knows how to use the web but has no access to a computer, as there's always a long queue to use the few that the school provides. Sometimes she and Karma Yogini go to a cybercafe in town to send emails, but not often.)

The fashion schools we find all charge high fees of several thousand Australian dollars. She shakes her head. She couldn't possibly ask her family for that sort of money.

I send an SOS to a friend who works at fashion magazine *marie claire* in Sydney, telling her of Karma Chokyi's plight. She emails back that a parcel of magazines is on its way.

One afternoon after school finishes, Karma Chokyi takes me on a tour and we peer through the window of her classroom. It looks like a lovely place to spend the day. Apart from the beautiful Bhutanese-style architecture of the buildings and the extraordinary view the students must have each day of the valley and the mountains, the walls are covered in homilies about learning and caring for each other.

They don't just learn basic literacy and languages here. Standard subjects in the Bhutanese curriculum include agriculture, environment, health, hygiene, population and 'moral science'. The government provides textbooks free to every student, most of them printed on the Taba family's press at Phuntsoling.

Conservation and the environment are also taken very seriously and students study it from primary school right through to college. The World Wildlife Fund has helped with an environmental studies program at Sherubtse College in eastern Bhutan and conducts environmental workshops and training programs on campus.

＊

After Karma Chokyi and Karma Yogini head off to school, the house moves into a new rhythm as the maids set about their weekly chores. There are floors to wash – by hand, on their knees with a bucket and a rag – chillies to dry, wool to sort, pumpkin seeds to dry in the sun and always washing to do.

When I first arrived Karma Yangki told me to leave my dirty washing outside my door for the maids to collect. This seemed way too much to ask. They were already doing so much for me with my meals and looking after Kathryn. The least I could do was my own washing. But they were determined to give me the full guest treatment, as I was to discover.

After a few days I noticed some of my clothes lying out on the roof in the sun. Someone (the maids, I assume) had taken what I'd been wearing the previous day and removed it from my suitcase to wash. After this happened a few times I relented and left some of my dirty washing outside my door. Everyone was much happier.

The Bhutanese use their roofs for drying all sorts of things. The sun at this altitude is stronger, with less atmosphere to penetrate. Despite the cold, if the sun is out then clothes, jumpers, even the doonas, can be washed and dried in one day on the reflective tin roof.

One of the most distinctive sights throughout the country is fresh, plump, bright red chillies. They are drying on the roofs, hanging from eaves or sitting in huge piles ready to be stored. They are everywhere and the Bhutanese eat them with everything. One of their most popular dishes, *emmadatshi*, is just chilli and a bit of cheese, cooked together and eaten at almost every meal.

The maids have different jobs each day of the week so while I work at the dining table, various activities go on around me, below or outside in the concrete front yard. Today I am distracted by Kathryn's squeals of delight coming from outside.

Standing close to the window I see her on a rug below, being entertained by Madonna while Wesel Wangmo looks on. The maids are washing the two kittens in a bucket of soapy water. They laugh at how comical the cats look, all wet and forlorn. A couple of stray dogs (an epidemic all across Bhutan) hover at the top of the driveway. They barked all night, keeping many in the household awake. The Bhutanese maid has no time for them and throws a rock every so often, which scares them away, for a little while.

Karma Yangki pops up the stairs and apologises that lunch today will be late and simple. It arrives in four copper containers, lined up on the table just for me. Cabbage and potato garnished with chervil; carrot and pumpkin soup; fish stew and red rice; followed by sliced apple and orange. There is bottled mineral water plus a flask of hot water. Simple? I am embarrassed anew – they completely spoil me with their boundless hospitality. I am certain Karma Yangki would stop apologising if she could see what passes for lunch at my place – a sandwich made from whatever is in the fridge.

Kathryn has her meals downstairs but whenever Wesel Wangmo thinks she needs breastfeeding or a sleep, she brings her back to me. It's lovely to have her so close that I can hear her and just wander down to say hello when I miss her, which usually happens at various points throughout the day.

The first morning Kathryn spent downstairs, three-year-old Madonna came up asking for a baby T-shirt, which I gave her. She reappeared a few minutes later stamping her foot, her little face creased with frustration. 'Baby T-shirt, baby T-shirt,' she kept demanding. It took a few minutes before I realised she was saying, 'Baby did shit.' It was a fresh nappy she was asking for. Once we sorted that out she became a useful go-between. Now Wesel Wangmo sends her upstairs asking for a 'baby napkin' and I send her back armed with a supply.

Sometimes as I work I can hear a little girl crying. It comes from the house behind us. The sisters tell me that shortly after the girl was born, her mother left for America, where she has a job as a nanny. It was meant to be for a short time but after three years she still hasn't returned. The little girl is being raised by her father but as he is at work during the day, her grandmother keeps an eye on her while she weaves at her loom. The little girl is lonely and frustrated at being cooped up all day. Often Renee will go down and bring her back here to play.

✳

One weekend we rug up and all go for a walk – Kathryn, Wesel Wangmo, Karma Chokyi, Madonna and I. Taba is on the outskirts of Thimphu and within a few minutes the houses come to an end. The countryside is wild and unspoiled, and although the trekking in Bhutan is among the best in the world, it is not really suited to an afternoon stroll, so we walk along the road.

Kathryn is in her high-tech stroller, which converts into a backpack. The way she likes to sit in it is stretched out like a starfish. She loves it and waves her arms and legs while screaming 'ya ya ya!' as loudly as she can. It looks pretty comical and she used to draw a lot of stares in Sydney. In Bhutan they are positively agog, and cars slow down as people do a double take.

The feeling is mutual – I am mesmerised by the traffic that passes me on the road. A man walks towards Thimphu wearing a *gho*, knee-high socks and carrying an impossibly heavy load of logs on his back. I stare at him staring at Kathryn. Another man in a dirty green *gho* and bare feet pulls a reluctant horse behind him. An army truck full of singing children overtakes us. They are returning to school after a day of dancing practice at the Changlimathang Stadium, where they will be performing for the King in a few days.

We cross the bridge in front of the Queen Mother's palace, nod to the guard, who stares at Kathryn like she's from another planet, and climb down beside the bridge to toss rocks into the water. The river, which starts high in the mountains, is arctic green, beautifully clear and frigid. It is autumn and around us the trees are turning various coppery shades.

We walk slowly back to Taba, just as the junior school finishes its day. Soon we are surrounded by young children in their uniforms. A few doors from home we come upon a crowd of schoolchildren staring into the front garden of a Taba neighbour. We join them. Two little blonde girls, aged about four and seven, are playing with dolls. They are an incongrous sight. The eldest enjoys the scrutiny and plays up to the crowd, arranging the doll on a window ledge. Her sister is shyer, sitting with her back to the crowd and her head down.

An American family lives here, Wesel Wangmo tells me. The father has some sort of job in agriculture. There are two daughters and an older son. Wesel Wangmo goes on to say, without a trace of self-consciousness or embarrassment, that when Karma Yangki heard there was a son in the family she phoned to ask him if he wanted a date with Wesel. Karma Yangki was surprised by the voice on the telephone and asked how old he was. He said fourteen. She told him that was too young. He became indignant and said he didn't think fourteen was too young at all and that he would love to go on a date. Wesel Wangmo and Karma Chokyi have no problem with Karma Yangki's behaviour. It's the boy they laugh at. I try to imagine myself being as good humoured if my older sister had phoned around trying to set me up on dates.

❋

When we get back to the house, the maids have tea ready. Kathryn and I have a little sleep then, just as she wakes, Wesel Wangmo appears to take her off downstairs. She has the un-canny ability to sense when Kathryn is awake, which is quite unnerving. I know I am alone upstairs – the floorboards creak whenever anyone walks anywhere – and yet after a few little gurgles from Kathryn, Wesel Wangmo is up the stairs and standing in the doorway.

I start to miss Kathryn so wander downstairs, following the sound of her cooing. I find almost the whole family piled into Karma Yangki's bedroom, as is so often the case. The TV is on and the Martin Scorsese film *Kundun* is playing on Indian cable. Karma Yangki is ironing. Kathryn is sitting in the middle of the bed playing with the delicious fried corn flakes that the Bhutanese eat as a snack. She has up-ended the bow and is happily spreading the flakes across the bedspread.

No-one seems particularly concerned. Renee is asleep on a pillow. Wesel Wangmo and Karma Chokyi are sitting on the floor by a vertical electric heater watching the movie. They make room for me on the mat and I slide on in.

Madonna is potty training and comes in wearing her mother's knickers, which hang off her little three-year-old hips. As far as she is concerned, they look the same and feel the same as her new underpants, so she can't understand why they keep falling down whenever she takes a step. Everyone howls with laughter.

Phuntsho Wangmo rings to say she will leave Renee here at Taba for the night and collect her in the morning. It has been a long day chasing film rushes, changing flights for different members of the foreign crew and dealing with the rest of the daily minutiae that is her job as production secretary. Renee bursts into tears, so Karma Yangki throws her arms around her and Madonna stands by stroking her leg.

But Renee is inconsolable. She wants her mum. Karma Yangki calls back her sister and Phuntsho Wangmo reassures Renee she will be here soon.

Kundun finishes and Karma Chokyi changes the channel to a Hindi soapie and turns down the volume. No-one pays any attention but they leave it on because it is not long until the Bhutanese Broadcasting Service begins transmission at 7pm.

Phuntsho arrives and Renee throws herself into her arms. They will both stay the night – in the double bed with Karma Yangki and Madonna. They often stay when Tenzin and Mani Dorji are at the family presses in Phuntsoling.

At 7pm, Wesel Wangmo switches the channel over, turns the volume up, and all conversation ceases. The BBS is about to begin. For a moment the screen is blank, then it bursts to life with opening shots of the handsome King surrounded by his adoring subjects. We see footage of the King out and about, attending to his regal duties. Then it's a few words from some friendly sponsors.

First a tyre shop. 'Cars, tractors, trucks. Come here for the best tyres in Thimphu,' someone promises in English. It is done with slides, like Australian TV in the '60s.

Then there's an advertisement for a clothing shop that sells, among other things, polar fleece jumpers, pants and jackets. I've been to that shop and it's packed wall to wall with cartons of clothing to sort through. But what it lacks in display it makes up for in price – about one-tenth of what the moun-taineering shops charge in Australia and America. Most of that clothing is made in Bangladesh or China. The manufacturers send any excess over the border here to Bhutan and it's out-rageously cheap.

The next commercial is far more sophisticated. It shows a man running into a shop in Thimphu and stealing a TV from a row of half-a-dozen on a counter. A 'policeman' gives chase, catches him and orders him to put his hands on his head and do squats, which he does. (This is obviously a peculiarly Bhutanese form of punishment. The only thing hurt is your pride. Most undignified – I'm with Karma Chokyi.) An English voiceover delivers the punchline: you don't have to steal at this shop to get a bargain on Sony televisions.

This style of advertising is new here and the BBS has just started offering to help businesses make their own advertise-ments. As yet only a few have been brave enough to try.

Finally, it's time for the news. A man and a woman, all feline good looks and high cheekbones, read from an autocue, first in Dzongkha then in English. It is a mixture of international, regional and local news. I am riveted. It is like another window is thrown open on this curious country, providing a fascinating glimpse into what is going on.

First up is the robust, pink-cheeked face of Bhutan's Minister for Health and Education, Sangay Ngedup. For the past two weeks, wearing a *gho* and a backpack, this jolly Cabinet minister has travelled the length and breadth of the country to reach people in the most remote corners and urge them to exercise. Surely it could only happen in Bhutan.

He covered all 560 kilometres on foot using what they

laughingly call their 'passports' – sturdy, muscular calves. The terrain is so mountainous and rugged that without a healthy set of those, no Bhutanese will get very far.

Next is a story on the inaugural Mountain Women of the World conference held in Thimphu. As part of the 2002 Year of the Mountain celebration, 250 women came from thirty-five countries including Scotland, Switzerland, Kyrzstan, Peru, France and Nepal to talk mountain business. There are fabulous shots of hundreds of women in various exotic traditional dress, from the ponchos of the American Appalachian women to what looks like a sheep draped around another woman's shoulders. (Peru perhaps? Uzbekistan?) They all grin happily together for the camera. It appears to be a fun conference, but how the women from Italy managed to communicate with their sisters from Tibet is anyone's guess.

The conference brought together mountain women, media, entrepreneurs, politicians and the interestingly named 'heroines'. (I'm not sure who they are but feel impressed all the same.) By all accounts it was a rip-roaring success and the Thimphu Declaration, which they all signed, is the result. It calls on the international community to recognise the strength and needs of mountain women everywhere.

Next there are more shots of the royal family, and what they got up to today, plus an update on the gold-smuggling racket that is the talk of Thimphu. It is a scandal unlike anything Bhutan has ever experienced and the country is aghast at the extent of the corruption and how long it has been going on. They think it is more like a Hindi soapie than what they expect of their own people.

Bhutan was the last country in the world to get TV. After centuries of shunning everything modern from beyond its borders, at his Silver Jubilee on 2 June 1999, the Dragon King stood before his people and announced that transmission would begin. 'But not everything you will see will be good,' he warned. 'It is my sincere hope that the introduction of television will be beneficial to our people and country.'

Overnight, cable television was made available, offering forty-six channels. Connection costs 1500 ngultrim (A$55) and a monthly subscription fee of 200 ngultrim (A$7.50). To counteract some of the outside influence, the King launched the national broadcaster, BBS.

I have seen the sisters watch Oprah and various Hollywood movies but they aren't that fussed about either. The enormous amount of Indian shows that are available on the cable channels seems to annoy them. The Bhutanese have a love–hate relationship with the country that wraps around two-thirds of their border.

Indian visitors must register but don't require that all-important, hard-to-get visa that other nationalities must have. Bhutanese can work in India, and there is a long tradition of Bhutanese studying in India and importing their teachers. A lot of business is done between the two countries. In fact Bhutan's two major exports are cement and electricity to India.

But the Bhutanese are fiercely protective of their own culture and wary of Indian influences. It's hardly surprising they feel vulnerable: India has more than a billion people while Bhutan has just 700 000.

TV has opened up a world they didn't know existed – Oprah, World Wrestling and *Buffy the Vampire Slayer*. But in some ways the more they see, the more fiercely protective they feel about their own culture.

Seeing the mess the rest of the world is in has reinforced the national trait of wanting to retain their own values and humble ways. At least that's how it is in this Taba household and among most of the educated, middle-class people I meet in Thimphu.

The best thing on TV as far as this family is concerned is the BBS news. And after watching it with them, I'd have to agree.

11

Twelve Eminent Men

Mal is back, commandeering the telephone and the formal lounge room for film business. But just as he lays out all his files and papers over two tables and connects the printer to his laptop, we are booted out. Bollywood is moving in. Or at least the Bhutanese equivalent.

A video crew is coming today, says Karma Chokyi over her shoulder, racing past while we eat breakfast. She is red-cheeked with excitement.

The whole household is abuzz and it takes us most of the morning to piece together exactly what is going on. It turns out that a video crew drove past a few days ago and liked the look of the front verandah – it is just what they need for a romantic scene in their movie. They are a little disappointed that the entrance doesn't have gates, which they feel are necessary for that extra touch of grandeur, but believe they can make do. They will film the Taba verandah and add footage of imposing gates from another home.

They also like the idea of the formal lounge room. It reflects just the right sense of sophistication for the wealthy young Bhutanese woman in their story.

Mal and I move all his producer stuff into a spare bedroom and sit side by side on the mattress on the floor. Kathryn sits opposite us playing with her vast range of toys: an empty plastic container, thermos lid and spoons.

All morning, sisters and maids rush past giggling, fussing around the verandah and lounge room and calling out to each other. Karma Yangki is wearing make-up (which is rare) and has a pretty pink shawl draped around her shoulders. Wesel Wangmo has donned a western-style dress I've not seen before, but the other sisters tease her so much she changes back into her everyday *kira*.

Mal and I are served lunch early, just after 11, and the dishes are quickly cleared away. Outside we can see the maids and sisters gathered in the driveway, ready to greet the star, or the 'hero' as they call him. The Bhutanese video industry is small and relatively new. This actor stars in almost every production.

Kicking myself that I have to leave in the middle of such showbiz excitement, Mal and I drive into town with Kathryn to buy new nappies. If it wasn't that Kathryn is actually wearing the very last one of the 120 nappies I brought with me, there is no way we would be going anywhere. But this is about as close to an emergency as it gets so Mal, Kathryn and I take off in Phuntsho Wangmo's little Maruti.

Driving in Bhutan is fun. Beautiful scenery, lots of sweeping bends and a leisurely pace. And not so many rules. Kathryn doesn't have to sit on her own, strapped into a baby seat in the back. There are no such things as baby seats or capsules here. Instead she sits up front on my knee watching the world go by. It's a little nerve-wracking at first and I wrap my arms tightly around her in case we round a corner and meet a stray cow, but it is also much more entertaining. Whenever Mal changes gears she leans forward and copies him.

At one point we're forced to stop for a herd of cows in the

middle of the road and groups of schoolchildren come up to the window to stare at Kathryn.

When we reach the supermarket, I am delighted to find it's well stocked. We buy enough supplies to fill the Maruti's boot, including bottled mountain water, which we go through very quickly in this dry mountain air, and disposable nappies from Japan and Thailand.

In the supermarket we bump into the only westerner I know in Thimphu – a kind New Zealand woman called Clare who was on my flight. She is the nearest thing to a guardian angel, having taken pity on me during the interminable delay in Kolkata Airport by buying me a cold beer and being gracious enough not to wince at the smell of vomit that surrounded me. She was travelling to Thimphu to meet her husband, who is on a project here with the Education Department.

I probably spoke to her for just two hours at the airport, but am wildly excited to see her and hear how she is getting on. While the shopkeeper packs our purchases into cardboard boxes – no plastic bags here – we chat and laugh like long-lost friends.

She is frustrated that after spending an hour typing an email at the local cybercafe, it all disappeared when she tried to send it. Apart from that little hiccup, she is having a lovely time. She and her husband have moved into a comfortable apartment in Thimphu, and while he has been away on brief trips out of town, Clare has been immersing herself in Thimphu life. We chatter away like excited schoolgirls, then go our separate ways, each happy to have found someone to marvel with about this amazing little country.

I realise my excitement is partly because I've hardly seen another westerner since arriving here. The tourists who come to Bhutan tend to come in trekking season – autum or spring – and then spend little time in the capital. The few westerners I have seen have been wearing suits and either lunching with Bhutanese businessmen or walking with them in the street, looking purposeful.

An extraordinary number of countries have business interests here. Japan sponsors road and agricultural projects. Germany is financing the restoration of an important *dzong*. Switzerland is helping train farmers in modern techniques. Denmark and Norway are involved in environmental schemes. Australia is involved in education, poultry, animal husbandry and study of the fruit fly. And so on. For a country with no significant global presence, it seems that a lot of countries are quietly volunteering their expertise to help in whatever way they can.

⁂

We head back and find that the 'hero' and 'heroine' still haven't arrived. There are some Jeeps outside the house and a couple of people with remote telephone handsets wandering around looking concerned. A woman sits on the verandah with a shoebox containing an eyelash curler, eye-shadow palette, brush and mirror. I guess she's the make-up department.

But the Taba household has given up waiting and gone back inside.

Finally at 5 pm, after hours of pacing and anxious phone calls, the crew call it a day. They tell us the weather wasn't good enough to film outside on the verandah. The real reason, the sisters tell us after they have gone, is that the heroine threw a wobbly – a star tantrum worthy of Hollywood. She didn't 'feel' up to filming today, so while everyone else waited around, she declined to appear. The video-makers are too embarrassed to admit that to us foreigners, in case we think badly of the Bhutanese.

In the evening the family go to the movies. There is a new Bhutanese video showing at Thimphu's Lugor Cinema and it stars the heroine who didn't turn up today. She is Bhutan's hottest actress, starring in most Bhutanese videos. She auditioned for the lead female role in Rinpoche's movie, but was passed over for Deki Yangzom, a beautiful but unknown, and completely inexperienced, young woman who works for the Royal Monetary Authority.

The sisters ask us if we would like to have dinner served in Karma Yangki's bedroom, where we can watch the TV. Another chance to watch the BBS news? You bet.

So Mal, Kathryn and I take up the most popular position in the house – on the mat by the bed. The maids bring dinner, followed by sweet tea.

After the BBS news, something is broadcast in Dzongkha. We don't understand a word but enjoy the strip advertisements in English that run across the bottom of the screen in one long, endless stream: apartment to rent in Bumthang . . . regrettable warning about an interruption to the power supply in some remote regional areas . . . job vacancies at the Royal Monetary Authority . . . Punakha Dzongkhag announces vacancies for 'a caretaker, sweeper, tractor driver and a ward boy' . . .

When the family returns, they give us their verdict on the movie. Thumbs down. It was about a monk who gets a girl pregnant. It was a mistake, yet he leaves the monkhood to marry her. But they aren't in love. Then he gets drunk and sells her and the child. Silly story, says Phuntsho Wangmo. But the heroine was good.

Hopefully the heroine will be in a more amenable mood tomorrow and the crew will be able to shoot her scenes at Taba. They don't reappear the next day, or the one after, and by the end of the week, as life moves on and Mal heads back up the yak trail, we've just about forgotten them.

※

The Taba house becomes the venue for a historic weekend in the middle of the month. It starts quietly enough, with the delivery on Friday morning of an enormous cardboard box. It's carried into the house by the driver of the delivery truck, the two younger sisters, a visiting male cousin and the two maids.

Whatever is in the box is heavy and the six of them struggle with it down the driveway to the front door. By the time I get up from the table and down the stairs to help, it is safely inside, standing on one end in the entrance foyer, and everyone has disappeared.

A few hours later, after lunch, sisters Karma Chokyi and Wesel Wangmo appear upstairs and start rearranging the furniture in the formal lounge room, opening the padlocked door of the shrine room and carrying things through. Young men arrive and place squares of carpet on some of the couches.

Karma Chokyi tells me that some people will be meeting here over the weekend, and they are getting ready for it. The way she says it, it doesn't sound like such a big deal but I take my laptop to bed and try to keep out of their way.

As the afternoon progresses, the tempo picks up, and by early evening the upstairs area is bustling. Half-a-dozen people are hard at work. A young man nails to the walls Buddhist paintings of various deities. Carpets from the lounge room are placed around the edges of the shrine room. The dining table is covered with a red tablecloth and then, lined up on it, a dozen enormous beaten copper pots with individual burners. The dining area is being transformed into an elegant banquet hall.

On the long table outside my bedroom a man sets up glasses and bottles of whisky, red wine and water, alongside Kathryn's baby formula. I whisk it away, then retrieve her pram from beside the front door. This is starting to look very big.

Phuntsho Wangmo and Tenzin Wangdi arrive after work, followed by Karma Yangki. They walk around the top floor inspecting everything, then disappear downstairs, deep in discussion. The maids place saucers with betel nut and lime leaves on low tables in front of each seat. Twelve places are set.

Karma Chokyi tells me the meeting is expected to start at around 9 the following morning and will probably go on till 5 pm. They will be in the lounge room but Karma Yangki doesn't want me to feel at all uncomfortable. I really should feel completely at home and come and go as I please, she insists.

On Saturday morning breakfast is early and the two maids are clearly preoccupied. They bring me a plate of toasted carrot, cabbage and tuna sandwiches, then rush off, gossiping to each other and giggling. Their excitement is contagious.

Determined not to be in the way, I eat quickly, have my bucket bath, forgo my warm fleecy trousers for a skirt and dig out the lipstick I know I packed, but haven't used since I got here. I do one last check that nothing of Kathryn's is on show anywhere and I'm back in my room by 8.30. There is a curtain across the bedroom door (as there is across every doorway in the house), which means I can leave the door open to hear everything, but stay discreetly tucked away.

Nine o'clock comes and goes and there is no sign of anyone. While sounds of activity float up from below, all around the top floor is a reverberating, expectant silence. After half an hour I can't stand it any more and venture downstairs.

It is bedlam. Happy, noisy, bedlam. And yet everyone seems quite relaxed.

The cardboard box that stood in the foyer yesterday has been moved into the living room and ripped apart. Emerging from its debris is one tall, freestanding tan-coloured two-door refrigerator – the finest one I have ever seen. The doors are still covered in their plastic wrapping, and Karma Yangki, Mani Dorji, Tenzin Wangdi and another man are putting an enormous trout in the vegetable crisper, then taking it out again, amid deep discussion.

Karma Yangki wishes me a cheery good morning as I pass. I ask if the men are expected soon and she just shrugs.

In the kitchen two new men, the sleeves of their *ghos* pushed up their muscular forearms, are working away beside the maids, who are giggling so much it's a wonder they can stand. Wesel Wangmo introduces a third man, the chief cook for the day. He is one of Thimphu's finest chefs, renowned for his haute cuisine, and has been hired for the weekend. He is gregarious and animated. In proud and near-perfect English he tells me the two maids are his helpers. They don't understand what he is saying but continue to buzz around him, clearly in awe of this accomplished man and willing to slice and dice and anything else he might require.

Pinned to the wall is the menu for the day. White rice, red rice, riverweed soup, pork fat with potato, *emmadatshi* (chilli with cheese), fried fish, beans, cauliflower, chilli beef, stewed yak, chicken, and more.

I head back to my room and sit up in bed with my laptop.

At 10.15 there is still no sign of the men. Karma Chokyi brings me a cup of tea and says, when I ask, that they will be here at about 11.

I realise I'm the only one doing any clock watching. Time is one of those notions we treat so differently. None of the sisters wears a watch and they don't refer to times in conversation, unless asked. Instead they leave such things vague and open-ended. Yet they manage to be on time when they need to be – for a movie or to catch an aeroplane. It's a mystery to me.

Karma Yangki drops by my room a quarter of an hour later and, in the same conversation, tells me two different times – 11.30 and 12.30. She doesn't seem to notice. Phuntsho Wangmo comes by and says definitely 12.15. Karma Chokyi still thinks 11.

At around midday I hear Karma Yangki and Phuntsho Wangmo laughing together at the top of the stairs, about the cook. Apparently he's complaining that the Bhutanese are always very late. With great indignation, he is telling anyone who will listen that foreigners are *sooo* much better to cook for because they always arrive exactly on time. These men are on Bhutanese time, the sisters tell me, laughing again. They are clearly not the least bit fussed.

Finally, between 1 and 1.30 pm, they arrive – twelve of Bhutan's most eminent and learned scholars, comprising the royally appointed Dzongkha Committee. It turns out that this weekend's 'meeting' is a conference, the culmination of years of work developing the national language.

The committee includes a judge, the head of the Royal

Advisory Council, the Director of Education, a doctor of traditional medicine and host, Mani Dorji. As owner of the largest private printing press in the country, he will be the dictionary's publisher. What they decide in the course of today and tomorrow will become fact and linguistic law for the whole kingdom.

In this country of less than a million people there are three official languages (English, Dzongkha and Nepalese) plus dozens of dialects, none of which have a written form. Many villages are so isolated and their dialects so diverse that much of the country doesn't understand each other. The language my adopted family speaks, Sharchop, is spoken in villages in the east. The Sharchop people are recognised as the original inhabitants of Bhutan and many have moved west to Thimphu.

As part of his vision to unify his kingdom, the previous king decided that a national language was needed. He chose Dzongkha, spoken by about a quarter of the population. The language had no written form so the first step was to create an alphabet and a style. Taking the Tibetan script that is used in Bhutanese monasteries, the Dzongkha script was developed. Some say it is the same as Tibetan, others insist it is more elegant. The official dictionary, to be finalised this weekend, is another step in the language process. It will provide the definitive guide to everything Dzongkha.

The men look wonderfully dignified and important, each one dresssed in the traditional *gho*. But as this is a gathering in Mani Dorji's home rather than an official state occasion, they aren't wearing the *kabney*, a three-metre long, ninety-centimetre-wide scarf draped over one shoulder and tied, just so. And because it isn't winter yet – that starts officially sometime in December, when the monks move to lower ground – the men all sport bare legs and long socks. Once the monks make their annual migration to Punakha (a village three hours' drive away and a lot warmer), the men of Thimphu can cover their legs, wearing tights or thermal long johns, much like I have on under my long woollen skirt, along with my thick woollen socks. I wonder how cold all those bare knees must be.

On the low tables in front of each man is the saucer of lime and betel nut, a china mug with sweet tea and a lid, and a thick red A4 folder full of words elegantly drawn in script, ready for their deliberations.

Karma Yangki tells me again that I am welcome to join the men at any time. Much as I would love to be a fly on the wall, I can't imagine I would be much help with a Dzongkha dictionary. (I'm not sure I would be much help on an English one, for that matter.)

Phuntsho Wangmo tells me that it's a shame they aren't talking in English because I would find it very interesting. I insist I'm not feeling at all left out, that I understand that if they are doing a dictionary of Dzongkha, it makes sense for them to conduct their discussions in Dzongkha.

She then asks if I would take photos of the occasion. I'm no photographer but would feel rather impolite admitting that right now, so instead I check my lipstick, make sure my thermal-covered ankles aren't visible, grab my camera and timidly venture in. Meetings in boardrooms with people called Packer had nothing on this. I feel I am witnessing something akin to our forefathers writing the constitution. I just hope I can stop trembling enough to focus the camera.

Fortunately I'm greeted by a kind-faced man I recognise, who immediately puts me at ease. He is Lungtaen Gyatsho, one of those charismatic men who appeared in the magic-school scene of Rinpoche's movie. He played the teacher, and ensuring his availability was crucial in the scheduling of the film.

When Mal worked out the shooting schedule he had to work around three fixed dates: the rice harvest in Paro Valley, the school exams of a fifteen-year-old student who plays one of the leads, and the diary of this very important man. As well as chairing the Dzongkha Committee, Lungtaen Gyatsho is involved in drafting the kingdom's first constitution. Dressed in robes, he is bald and portly, with a square face, tinted wire-rimmed glasses and a goatee.

While I wait, camera at the ready, he makes a short speech. I understand a few words – writer, Australia, husband, Rinpoche, photo, which pretty much explains why I am standing in their midst – and I nod every time I recognise a word.

I write novels in Australia. My 'husband' is producer of Rinpoche's new film. And I am about to take their photo.

The men respond with huge smiles and nods. I suspect that has more to do with their respect for Rinpoche and the huge interest in his film than me, my job or nationality – given that they don't have fiction writers and little from Australia makes the 7 o'clock BBS news.

As I happily record this slice of Bhutanese history, moving around the room photographing each man, the reactions range from stern-faced and proud to grinning down the lens. One man says he has to show his teeth then flashes a huge smile. I tell him he has great teeth and he laughs with delight. Snap. Another gentleman strikes a pose of grave dignity, holding it so rigidly, not even a hair would dare to move. Snap.

Photos taken, I shuffle my way out the door, part-bowing, part-genuflecting, back to my bedroom, leaving them to get on with the important stuff. I'm sure this isn't how the *Oxford Dictionary* was written, but there you go. The Bhutanese do everything in their own delightful way.

From my cosy workstation sitting up in bed, I hear raucous laughter, then silence. It's impossible to work with this going on a few metres away. Way too exciting. I just wish I understood Dzongkha.

I'm invited to join the dignitaries for lunch so I line up with them at the sumptuous buffet. While helping himself and me to yak stew, one man explains that Dzongkha is a very difficult language that is still developing. While there is much laughter coming from the room, there is also much earnest discussion as they struggle with meanings. Their job is also to agree on new Dzongkha words for modern western concepts such as 'computer' and 'internet'. They believe it is important for their culture to have its own equivalents. At present the English words are accepted parlance, but only until there is a Dzongkha word and it appears in the dictionary.

Not everyone in Bhutan agrees that new words are necessary. Some believe that most Bhutanese already know the English words and they should be accepted. Others say Dzongkha is difficult enough without creating new terminologies. But the Dzongkha Committee believes it is crucial for the development and continuing survival of the new national language that it be thoroughly Bhutanese.

As Lungtaen Gyatsho puts it: 'If we take every new idea and term in its original English form, Dzongkha in a decade will be overloaded with foreign words. And one day Dzongkha may fail to qualify and justify itself to be Bhutanese.' However, words pertaining to international standards of measurement, like kilogram, kilometre, Fahrenheit and Celsius, will stay the same.

The idea of creating new words is fascinating and I ask as many questions as I can fit in while these eminent men pile their plates with food.

One man explains that the committee receives lists of English words it needs, with suggestions for a new Dzongkha word. A judicial representative provides a list of legal terms that are in use and his suggestions for a Dzongkha word. An education bureacrat provides education terms, the medical fraternity gives medical terms, and so on. The committee generally accepts their recommendations. Otherwise they set about creating their own. They do this by painstakingly breaking down the English term to its root and following the development of its meaning. Then, if possible, they follow the same line of reasoning to coin their new Dzongkha word. My brain starts to ache at the thought of the discussions that are going on inside that room and my respect grows for these men and their scholarly abilities.

All too soon I reach the end of the table, where there are two small bowls. These, I'm told, are for me. Karma Yangki was concerned that I might find the rest of the buffet too hot so asked the maids to prepare two vegetable dishes without chilli, just for me.

The thoughtfulness of this family is almost overwhelming. I'm no dignitary, nor a paying guest. When Mal dropped me – and my baby – on their doorstep I was a complete stranger from the other side of the universe. Nevertheless I'm a guest and it is the Bhutanese way to show every possible kindness. Adoring my baby for large chunks of the day while I work isn't enough. They think of everything.

The chilli dishes created for the dignitaries are indeed hot. That burn-the-roof-of-your-mouth-and-never-speak-properly-again kind of hot. I like chilli and thought I could tolerate it pretty well. But these dishes bring new respect. Wow.

No-one else seems perturbed and I realise that for the past two months, the maids have been toning down the chilli in all my meals.

Just after lunch has been served, the chef is called away urgently. His usual employer has to travel unexpectedly to the other side of Bhutan tomorrow and the chef must prepare for the journey. He races out the door in a flurry, hands waving.

Karma Yangki and Phuntsho Wangmo are sorry to see him go. Not only was he supposed to prepare lunch and dinner again tomorrow, but he was a funny man, they say. He prides himself on his good English, boasting to them that he speaks it better than his two children who learn it at school. While chopping and dicing he chatted away to Kathryn in English but became offended when she wouldn't reply. Wesel Wangmo had to explain that she ignores her parents too. At nine months she doesn't speak English to anyone.

As he drives away, two cars pull up and park at the top of the driveway. Two heavily made-up young Bhutanese women, looking very glamorous, step out of the cars, followed by a couple of young men. It's the film crew. They're back. I point them out to Karma Yangki, expecting her to be horrified, or at the very least annoyed. 'Oh no, not today,' she says mildly, which I think may be as stressed as she gets.

Phuntsho Wangmo goes out to talk to them. The most glamorous of the young women, presumably the lead actress, stands slightly apart from the group, obviously listening to everything being said. I feel sure a hissy fit is looming.

Phuntsho Wangmo returns, and she and Karma Yangki have a chat. Karma Yangki is firm. She told the video people that they could shoot here, so they can. While the upstairs formal lounge is occupied, they can shoot downstairs and on the verandah. When the dignitaries leave at 4 o'clock, the film crew will move into the formal lounge room. The producer/director is relieved. After seeing inside last week, he has his heart set on this house. As far as he is concerned, it has the best verandah and formal lounge in Thimphu. Down the driveway they come – the hero, the heavily made-up heroine, old man, young woman, cameraman and the producer.

While the Dzongkha Committee creates a standard of litera-ture for the kingdom's future, the film crew and all their hangers-on flit between the downstairs thoroughfare and the upstairs verandah. Somehow it will all work. And of course, it does.

The film crew take up positions in Karma Yangki's bed-room and are instantly absorbed into the day, sitting on the floor by the bed, taking tea, and helping to entertain Kathryn. The make-up artist works on the heroine, adding yet another layer of foundation and eye shadow.

After lunch the men get back to business while downstairs the film crew gets ready to roll. The video-makers don't mind an audience – which is fortunate because as well as their own hangers-on they now have myself, Kathryn, the two maids and the four sisters all huddled in different corners watching them set up.

The producer has spotted the family's fancy new refriger-ator, standing proudly in the living room, and decides that it's perfect for a scene they had intended to film at another location. They arrange some copper pots – the same ones that have just fed the dignitaries – along one wall to create the appearance of a kitchen in an upper-class home. The room is directly below the formal lounge room and a low murmur of voices is vague but audible. It doesn't appear to worry the producer.

Barely have they shot one frame before it grinds to a halt. Much animated discussion ensues between hero, heroine and producer. The cast isn't getting along. The younger sisters whisper translations of what is being said, their eyebrows raised. They thought the actress was very good in the movie they watched at the Lugor Cinema but they're most unimpressed with her 'attitude' (which they consider very Bollywood). Culturally the Bhutanese love to tease and be teased. They don't take themselves too seriously and it's not often someone is allowed to develop a big head. The attitude of this temperamental diva is considered very un-Bhutanese.

In the video they are making today she plays a scheming sister-in-law, which they say is very Hindi, and not at all reflective of Bhutanese life. This offends the sisters. Tired of the Hindi soaps on cable TV and all the Bollywood films that play at the Lugor Cinema, they want to see Bhutanese stories.

Kathryn is ready for a nap so we return to our room and I'm sitting up in bed with my laptop again when one of the dignitaries drops by on his way to the bathroom. He is Bhutan's top translator of Dzongkha to English and vice versa, and tells me sadly that he was rejected by an Australian university for a postgraduate diploma in translation because Dzongkha isn't taught there. He asks if I have any relatives connected with the university. In Bhutan, family is the backbone of everything and, by extension, also the way of business. Given that Thimphu has a population of just under 50 000, almost everybody is related somehow, and here that would be a perfectly reasonable question.

He explains he wants to translate valuable and treasured Bhutanese Buddhist texts into English for the next generation of Bhutanese and for people in the west, who are showing an interest. A worthwhile ambition, I think. He wants to sharpen his translation skills and already has the support of the Royal Business Council.

I promise him that while I don't have any family at the university, I will see what I can find out and we swap email addresses.

The men work all afternoon while filming goes on downstairs. Somehow the two coexist. The dictionary is coming along beautifully and the Dzongkha Committee decides it would like to continue working into the early evening. No problem, says Karma Yangki.

This means a delay for the film crew being able to use the lounge room. They decide they will do the balcony shots while they wait.

It also means conjuring up dinner for twelve, this time without a chef. The sisters roll up their considerably long traditional sleeves and get cooking. While Karma Yangki, Wesel Wangmo and the maids start chopping in the kitchen, I join the production line set up on the floor in the living room. We're making *momo*s. A bamboo tray of small, flat, round dough pieces is passed around.

Karma Chokyi and Phuntsho Wangmo show me how to place a piece on the palm of the hand, add a dollop of filling, then swivel it to create a little dim sim with a fancy spiral top. Theirs are neat and stylish, each one with a perfect decorative whirl. Mine look like a molten heap. They don't mind, and place them alongside their own.

Another feast is produced with little fuss and much laughter – white rice, red rice, deep-fried hard-boiled eggs, *japati*s, cheesy potato with dill, maize, *dhal*, red *emmadatshi* and magnificently styled *momo*s.

※

The VIPs line up again at the buffet and they too can't resist a peek through the curtains to see what's going on outside on the verandah. They then take their plates back into the lounge room to continue their discussions. The sisters and I quickly take their place, peeking through the curtains. The actress smiles good-naturedly back at us.

As the sun disappears behind the mountains, the last vestiges of warmth go too. Almost instantly, it is freezing but she doesn't complain. She turns out to be quite the trooper, sitting patiently while the producer and cameraman set up lights and decide on the right angle. Finally they give the nod. She whips the shawl from around her shoulders and she is *her*. The evil, scheming sister-in-law entertaining her lover on the elegant terrace. She pours tea. Cut. The tea doesn't pour. There's a blockage in the mouth of the thermos. They fix it and try again. The camera rolls. Cut. The actress can't get the hang of the thermos. And so it goes on, take after take.

Finally the Dzongkha committee winds up, due back on the job at 10 o'clock tomorrow morning. The men file past the film crew, who are freezing as yet again the verandah scene goes wrong. The producer decides to abandon it as the best lounge room in Thimphu has just become available. But his lead actress is too cold to continue and nothing can persuade her. With a heavy sigh, the producer tells Karma Yangki they will be back next week.

As they depart and the household is finally preparing for bed, Mal arrives from location, with rushes to be couriered urgently to Bangkok for processing. He is running on nervous energy and Karma Yangki kindly arranges for the maids to bring us tea. It's been days since we have spoken and we catch up, sitting in the formal lounge room, surrounded by the hefty Dzongkha Committee folders that the men have left behind.

Mal will have to be up at 5 am to deliver the rushes to the airport at Paro, a few hours away. Just after dawn, the maids lay out a hot breakfast for him, tea for me and porridge for Kathryn, before starting preparations for another day and evening of dignitaries, gourmet buffets and no chef.

❋

The men of the Dzongkha Committee continue their discussions over lunch and right through dinner. Finally finished, they take a few moments to relax and open the bar. Some have scotch, others French red wine.

By the time the men leave, at about 9 o'clock on Sunday night, everyone in the household is exhausted. As the last pair of tail lights disappear up the driveway, the big four — Phuntsho Wangmo and husband Tenzin Wangdi, Karma Yangki and husband Mani Dorji — collapse on the couches in the lounge room, amid the debris of saucers with torn lime leaves, teacups and glasses. Mani Dorji shares some of what went on in the meeting. All in all, they think they hosted a successful conference. I agree. Even without understanding the Dzongkha, I think it was fabulous.

Karma Yangki chews on betel nut, the eastern delicacy that keeps you warm, gives a bit of a high and makes your teeth red. Bhutanese lipstick, she calls it, with a laugh. She seldom drinks but makes an exception tonight, and together she and I finish off a bottle of red wine. Kathryn is asleep in her bed and as she has just about weaned herself off my breastmilk, I feel no guilt. Mal comes home. The rushes made it in time and he has spent the rest of the day in the office. He is too exhausted to speak, swaying in the doorway before heading off to bed.

I'm not sure if it's the betel nut or the wine, but by the time Karma Yangki totters downstairs, her face is flushed rosy-red and she's doing a lot of giggling. It's been months since I have had a glass of wine and the effect is immediate. I'm lucky I don't have to negotiate stairs. A few steps and I'm face down on the bed, snoring in time with Kathryn and Mal.

✳

The following morning is Monday, the start of the week, and life in the Taba household starts to return to normal. Wesel Wangmo takes Kathryn downstairs and the maids serve Mal and me breakfast at the dining table. Mani Dorji's driver warms the car in the driveway while he waits for the boss to emerge.

And the phone rings for Mal. More crises. The most urgent one is that Penjore, the crusty old stall-holder who is required for the week's shooting, has gone missing. No-one can find him anywhere in Thimphu.

Mal fills in Karma Yangki on his latest dilemma. 'No problem Mal, we know the family,' she says, climbing into Phuntsho Wangmo's car and tucking her *kira* around her feet.

The sisters comb the city streets, visiting all his known haunts and dropping in unannounced on various relatives. His wife says sheepishly that he might be in Delhi, others say Phuntsoling, or maybe Khalingpong in India.

The search widens and family in villages all across Bhutan are contacted. No-one can give a clue to his whereabouts. The film schedule is rearranged and the art department create posters of his rugged face which they stick to trees along the main highway. His wife is more embarrassed than concerned about his safety, and it appears that Penjore just got cold feet and took off. The first month of shooting featured this man so it's a bit late to change actors.

After a few days the media is called in. The BBS news reports on the drama unfolding on the film, asking viewers to report if they have seen this man.

Almost a week passes, with the crew filming everything else possible. With no sign that Penjore will ever turn up, Rinpoche rewrites a crucial scene to exclude him. As he dictates the changes, the crew are surprised at how pleased he appears. After thinking about it overnight, Rinpoche has decided that Penjore's disappearance is a blessing. 'We didn't need that scene,' he announces. 'It's much better this way.'

Finally Penjore does show up on set, right towards the end, and Rinpoche spontaneously decides that a wood-chopping scene is required. He sets the actor to work, not letting him rest until he is satisfied.

12

The Wrap Party

LATE NOVEMBER 2002

The end of the film shoot is just a few weeks away and excitement is building for the wrap party. Well, it is among the women in the big house in Taba. It's the last thing on the minds of the cast and crew, who are still six hours up the road battling the rigours of filming and camping in icy conditions.

Mal has moved in to Taba full-time and is knee deep in the endless film dramas, which he juggles with admirable calm and efficiency from the family's formal lounge room. A long tangled telephone cord, hundreds of feet long, means the family phone can service upstairs and downstairs. When it's a call for Mal, which is most waking hours, it is carried up to him. When it's family business, which is also most waking hours, he carries it back down.

Every day or so Mal goes into the office behind the shops at the bottom of the main street in Thimphu. Kathryn and I sometimes drop by for lunch and it's always buzzing. If I thought it was a happening place before, the looming end of the shoot makes it more so. The two phonelines ring constantly, people drop by for a thousand different reasons, and a whiteboard on the wall is constantly being updated with a list of things to do.

This morning, Phuntsho Tobgey, a round-faced monk, who is assistant to the producers, is in town. Among other things he ferries people, film and supplies between Thimphu and the location. At the moment he is more interested in bouncing Kathryn on his knee. Beside him Phuntsho Wangmo is on the telephone chasing the previous week's rushes, which were unexpectedly offloaded in Bangkok by Druk Air.

Sitting in the office armchair – part of an old lounge suite relocated from the house at Taba – is Jo Juhanson, technical co-ordinator on the film. When he isn't making films, he is a volunteer firefighter in Sydney. The news from home hasn't been good. Bushfires are ringing New South Wales and Canberra. He is anxious, feeling that he should be there, working alongside his mates to fight the fires. He will happily miss the wrap party and is waiting for Phuntsho Wangmo to get him on an earlier flight out.

Most of the sixteen foreigners want their travel arrangements changed. Circumstances at home may mean they want to leave earlier than planned, others want to stay on after the film finishes and see a bit of Bhutan, and another has decided to travel out of Bhutan by road into India, then catch a train across the plains to fly out of Delhi. Between film crises, Phuntsho Wangmo handles all their travel plans.

For Phuntsho Tobgey and Jo Juhanson, the hubbub around them provides a welcome lull. The past week has been gruelling for them.

An entire scene, shot at a remote hut during the first weeks of filming, is out of focus. The editors discovered it well after the crew had moved to the next location so rather than endure the expense and hardships of carting everybody and their equipment back into the forest, Phuntsho and Jo dismantled the hut and have reassembled it in an empty hall in

Thimphu. The crew will reshoot the hut interiors in the hall and, as long as the continuity department get everything exactly right, the audience should never know. Phuntsho and Jo have been hard at it for the past week, rebuilding the hut, placing every wooden plank exactly where it had been in the forest.

Oblivious to the level of noise in the office, the American location secretary, Noa, is in a quiet world of her own, sitting at one end of the three-seater sofa, laboriously collating photographs and the names of all the cast and crew into her computer to create a souvenir directory of contact details for them all to keep in touch. Many lasting friendships have been made during filming. It's a killer of a job and not least because the names are so confusing to a westerner. The film employs eight Karmas, seven Ugyens, three Sonam Dorjis, three Phuntshos (one male, two female) and countless Tashis, Jigmes and Pemas.

The art director and deputy art director are both called Ugyen Wangchuk. To distinguish them on the set they are referred to as 'Ugyen Wangchuk the monk' and 'Ugyen Wangchuk the elder'. The Bhutanese are bemused that the westerners find this so strange.

Today in the office one of the Sonam Dorjis, the one who is the location accountant, is going through receipts with Mal, who is sitting alongside Phuntsho Wangmo and sharing her already-crowded desk space. At the same time as Mal types rows of numbers into his laptop, he is trying to organise a famous musician to record some of his haunting music for backing tracks.

Jigme Drukpa, a lecturer at the Royal Academy of Performing Arts in Thimphu, is considered the country's pre-eminent traditional musician. He is very learned and his music is extraordinary but it is his enthusiasm that has endeared him to everyone on the film. He became well-known in Bhutan in the 1980s when he released an album of his own and others' folk songs. Undaunted by the lack of recording facilities in the country, he made 300 audio tapes by buying 300 cassettes and performing each song 300 times into a tape recorder. I kid you not.

Another singer (another Sonam Dorji) is recording a catchy little number called 'The Traditional Yak Song'. It tells the story of life through a yak's eyes. Kind of home on the range, but without the buffalo. The final verse, which deals with him going to the abattoir, has been sensitively left off. Once Sonam Dorji has recorded the traditional version, Australian musician Ben Fink, formerly of The Whitlams, will give it his special spin, producing a modern techno version – known as 'Yak Doof'.

Jigme is proficient on a host of weird-looking instruments, including the distinctive *dramyin*, a kind of traditional guitar made with animal hide and a long wooden neck that curves up into a dragon's head. A Bhute lute, you could say.

After the film finishes the affable Jigme will go back on the road collecting the oral musical history of the different regions.

In the midst of all this industry and organised chaos, Karma Yangki and Phuntsho Wangmo manage a bit of a chat about something vitally important. Their frocks for The Party. The wrap party is the talk of Thimphu and invitations are much prized. All 108 cast and crew members are invited, along with their partners, or one invited guest. The five principal cast members can invite two.

I discover that Karma Yangki has had her personal weaver working on a special *kira* for the past three months. *That's* how much of a big deal it is.

It's only as Karma Yangki says this that a small mystery is solved that has been niggling at the back of my brain since I moved into the house in Taba all those weeks ago. When I'm alone in the top of the house, working away at my laptop, I often hear a strange *ka-thump, swoosh, ka-thump, swoosh* sound. It is rhythmic and almost comforting, providing a background beat to typing. I've been meaning to ask what it is but only ever notice it when I'm alone and then forget when the sisters appear.

It turns out that the noise is made by Karma Yangki's personal weaver. I've never laid eyes on this woman but I find out that each day I've been here, she has been working away in a little shed at the front corner of the property. She sits at the foot of her traditional backstrap loom creating the centuries-old style of cloth that Bhutan is renowned for.

Weaving is a huge part of Bhutanese cultural heritage and it is not uncommon for a family's wealth to be held in the fine fabrics it has tucked away in trunks. It is common practice to give as gifts lengths of woven cloth that the recipient would then have made into a *kira* or *gho*.

Karma Yangki scoffs at my awe over the three months it is taking to weave the three panels for her party *kira*. Three months is nothing, she says. The truly elaborate ones can take up to a year (and cost around US$1000).

All Bhutanese girls learn the art of weaving but the wealthier families often have their own full-time weaver who works under the direction of the lady of the house, creating cloth for all their needs – *kira*s for the ladies, *gho*s for the men, cushion covers, bags, and cloth for gifts.

Fashions change and it is important to keep up. At festivals the women wear their very best *kira*s and check each other out, noting the various new designs. The weavers draw on a lengthy repertoire of traditional patterns. How they combine and reinterpret them reflects their personal sense of style and creativity. The patterns can look from a distance like embroidery but actually they are woven into the fabric using the finger or a slender pick made from something fine but sturdy, like a porcupine quill. Karma Yangki wants her *kira* to be vivid red with gold decorative warps and wefts incorporated into the 'ground' of the fabric.

Discovering the splendour of what Karma Yangki is planning sends me into a tailspin. All I packed is thermals, thermals and more thermals. Not an evening frock among them. She and Phuntsho Wangmo tell me not to worry. They will take care of everything.

Mal is also focused on the wrap party but in a different way. He needs to find the right venue. There needs to be good food, good wine and lots of music and dancing, but because Rinpoche will be there, it also needs to have some formality. It isn't that Rinpoche doesn't 'do' informal, it's because the Bhutanese feel such reverence and devotion for him that they'd feel uncomfortable. Foreigners may be relaxed and irreverent about such things but the Bhutanese are not going to let their hair down and shake their booty in the presence of such a highly revered reincarnate lama.

After visiting various venues around Thimphu, Mal books the ballroom at the elegant and upmarket Druk Hotel for a buffet dinner and speeches, and the nightclub next door for the party afterwards. The women will look elegant and traditional for the formal part of the evening, and can then change out of their *kira*s into their dancing clothes, to hit the nightclub. By all accounts, dancing in a *kira* is hard work.

※

The busyness of the office spills over into Taba. Phuntsho Wangmo and Mal often don't return until after 9 pm, with more work still to do. The pressure is relentless.

Mal works away on his laptop till the early hours every morning, doing paperwork, sending emails, organising accounts. He is back on the laptop and taking telephone calls by 9 am.

His face is grey and the combination of the bitterly cold nights on location, little sleep and high stress has brought on a bout of sinusitis. That toothache turned out to be a little more serious. He has suffered from sinusitis before and travels with antibiotics but his supply is exhausted. The symptoms have been getting steadily worse and every morning he complains that his face is on fire.

A week before the final scenes are shot, I'm woken in the middle of the night by whimpering. Half-dazed with sleep I feel around in the bed for Kathryn. I can hear her but can't find her. I push at Mal, fearing she's under him, and start to panic.

It is only when I come fully awake that I realise the whimpering isn't coming from under Mal – it *is* Mal. All six-foot-two of him is curled into a foetal position making the most gut-wrenching whimpering sounds. He is in agony.

Having woken me, he is concerned he'll wake Kathryn, so he struggles to his feet and stumbles into the lounge room to lie on a couch. Dawn is a few hours away and he spends the time thrashing around on the couch, white-faced with pain.

With morning comes some respite from the cold and his pain eases, but overnight more urgent film things have sprung up and before we finish breakfast the phone calls start. First up it's the location secretary with a new problem. Mal starts the day.

I go to see Karma Yangki. She is, as always, calm, concerned and ready to help in any way she can. She gets the phone off Mal and calls the doctor. Dr Pema Dorji, the doctor of traditional medicine who is part of the Dzongkha Committee, says he will be over as soon as he can (which is a bit like getting the surgeon-general to pop by for a house call).

He greets me like a long-lost friend and I take him into the bedroom where Mal, having dealt with the most pressing of his film matters, has passed out again. Dr Dorji spends a lot of time taking Mal's pulse, pressing three fingers into his wrist and gently moving them about. He doesn't check his watch as it isn't specifically speed or strength that he is listening for. It is *everything* about the pulse – the quality, cadence, flow, any sharp peaks, and its whole general feel. Then the two men talk about the pain, where it is, what it feels like, and so on.

Dr Dorji's bedside manner is gentle and jolly, and for the first time in days Mal manages a smile. He gives Mal three bags of different-coloured pills to take at specific times of the day.

Bhutanese traditional medicine is similar to Tibetan medicine and involves the integration of mind and body. Their theory incorporates knowledge culled from Chinese, Indian and Arabic–Greek practices that were shared in cross-cultural medical forums held as far back as the third century. Treatments include pulse diagnosis, acupuncture, specially prepared herbs and spices, diet, specific timings of medications throughout the day, plus mantra, meditation, sounds and other more esoteric methods.

Urine analysis also is important. It is best to provide samples first thing in the day, which is why clinics can be full of people in the morning and empty by afternoon. The doctors look at viscosity, odour, colour and content.

As word of Mal's condition spreads through the family, it sparks discussion about everybody else's ailments. Wesel Wangmo is on a course of tablets that she is meant to take before dawn. She is finding it tough to follow because she keeps waking too late to take that first pill.

Sometimes the medicines can be light-sensitive so need to be taken in the dark. The patient crushes them before bed, wakes before first light and takes them with warm water, getting straight back into bed and covering the body to stay warm. Phuntsho Wangmo suffers a skin rash on her hand and is on a course of tablets that prohibits her from having meat or alcohol.

Treatments are intended to work with the body and, contrary to western expectations (where we want to feel better immediately), can be slow to take effect. It may be at least a week or two before any improvement.

Before he leaves, Dr Dorji has a chat with Karma Yangki and she adjusts Mal's diet accordingly. Yak, aged cheese (ghastly, rancid, hard lumps, which they bury in the ground to age) and chilli are off the menu. Mal looks genuinely disappointed.

The morning of the party approaches and Mal is still in pain. He's a really unhealthy grey but can't slow down. He has dozens of things demanding his attention and they can't be put off or passed on to someone else. Film-making just doesn't work that way, particularly at this point in the schedule.

There is a deadline and a budget, and any deviation throws everything out.

Karma Yangki calls for me after lunch. We are to get dressed at Phuntsho Wangmo's place in town and we'll see Mal there. I have my doubts he is going to make it but wave goodbye to him anyway.

I crowd into the four-wheel drive with everybody else, only this time I beat Karma Yangki outside and score a seat in the back, leaving the front seat for her. It's where she would normally sit, but with me around, she always gives me the front seat. Today it's hers. There are five women across the back and two children. Throughout the trip Kathryn is passed along the back seat, then over to Karma Yangki and back again.

We head into the office and upstairs to Phuntsho Wangmo's apartment.

The afternoon is enormous fun – half-a-dozen of us dressing for the party and a few others there to help. The last time I got dressed with so many women was for my best friend's wedding fifteen years ago, and the excitement level is about as high.

Out come all the brightly coloured *kira*s, laid across the bed, all glorious and dramatic. Lined up beside each one is a silk blouse to be worn underneath, called a *wonju*. Each of these is made from single-colour silk, either a pale pastel or bold jewel colour. Then there is the bolero-style patterned silk jacket called a *toego* that is worn over the top. The possible combinations of these three garments provides an endless kaleidoscope of colour.

Karma Yangki pulls out a magnificent blue *kira*, which she intends to wear. I am confused.

'What happened to the beautiful red *kira* your weaver has been working on for the past three months?'

She smiles shyly and shakes her head. Phuntsho Wangmo explains that when Karma Yangki saw it finished she decided it was over the top. Too bold and dramatic.

Karma Yangki pulls it out of a bag to show me. She brought

it with her just in case at the last minute she did feel bold enough to carry it off. I see what she means. It is stunning. Vivid red with delicate gold detail. It is not a *kira* for the faint-hearted. Karma Yangki doesn't want to stand out and no amount of arguing will change her mind. It doesn't matter — she'd look good in a curtain and is absolutely gorgeous wearing the sky blue.

Once Karma Yangki is sorted, it is my turn. There are a few *kira*s, *wonju*s and *toego*s laid out on the bed for me to choose from. After much consultation and everyone voicing an opinion, it is decided what I should wear. It takes three of them to dress me, firstly in a vivid orange silk *wonju*, which is like a shirt but without buttons. They sort of tuck it into place. Then two of them drape me in an orange and green *kira*, pinning it at the shoulders with a pair of elaborate round gold brooches called *koma*s. Finally they wrap a long multicoloured cloth belt around my waist, very tightly, circling it many times and tying it at the back. Over the top of it all goes a shiny pale green *toego*, which also doesn't have buttons but is somehow tucked into place.

We're ready. Piling back into the four-wheel drive, we then speed off to go to the Druk Hotel in the centre of town.

⁂

As it turns out, every western woman on the crew is loaned a *kira* and shown how to wear it by her new Bhutanese friends. We make a self-conscious, gawky bunch. The Bhutanese women are petite and elegant, and make lovely swishing noises as they glide effortlessly across the floor. Some of the western women manage to carry it off but the rest (including me) look clumsy, even when standing perfectly still. I feel marooned inside all this fabric. I can barely breathe, let alone move.

All the men arrive wearing *gho*s. The western members of the crew have spent days being fitted and learning how to tie the belt just right to make the chest pouch. They wear them with varying degrees of grace. Some sit modestly with their knees together while others are legs akimbo, leaving us in no doubt about their preference for boxers or Y-fronts. That's at the start of the night. After a few wines it's as if they've metaphorically loosened their ties. Every single one of them. Except Mal. He's the only man not wearing a *gho*. He didn't have time to organise for one to be made, and being so tall and broad, was unlikely to find one his size in a shop. He arrives looking very dapper in a grey three-piece suit, a rosy glow and a beaming grin. He looks like a different man from the one I waved goodbye to a few hours earlier.

'Feeling better?' I ask.

'Yeah, I feel great,' he says, sweeping me up in the middle of the lobby to plant a big kiss. 'You look gorgeous.'

I'm immediately suspicious. Either that is a well-meaning lie or his judgment is seriously impaired. I saw a mirror and I *know* I look like a round wooden keg. *Kira* fabric is so stiff and heavy that I have doubled in size.

'Have you taken something?' I ask.

'Yeah, the last of the painkiller pills.'

And then he's gone, lost in a bear hug with a burly Bhutanese.

The unofficial guest of honour, at least among we residents of Taba, is the apple farmer who plays an apple farmer in the film. He has struck a chord with everyone. Rinpoche found him selling his fruit in Thimphu market. Ap Dochu is aged eighty-one (or thereabouts), small, wiry, with half-a-dozen teeth. Despite the best efforts of the director and crew, he never understood that he was playing a part in a movie and believed everything that was happening was real.

When the plot called for the truck to break down, he became agitated that it happened again and again, lamenting that it should occur just when Rinpoche needed it. When asked to sleep for a campfire scene, he did just that, snoring happily through take after take. After three weeks he was completely confused at the dithering and silliness that seemed to be surrounding him. Finally he boarded a bus heading for Thimphu, believing at last he was going home. Seconds later it stopped around the corner and backed up so that the crew could film it again, from another angle. He stamped his foot in frustration and complained that it took just four hours to get there but was taking days to get home.

When he arrives at the party there is a ripple of excitement and Karma Yangki brings him over to say hello. He has a lined face, twinkling eyes and wears an air of calm bemusement – which could be either his usual manner or how he has decided to approach another evening of silliness with these strange people. I ask Karma Yangki if he is enjoying the party and she shrugs. She has no more of an idea of what is going on in his head than I do. He doesn't speak Sharchop, English or Nepalese, her three languages. But like me, she is utterly capti-vated. So we stand and grin together, the three of us.

Mal is head and shoulders taller than everyone else in the room so wherever I am, I can see his head bobbing around, his face creased with a permanent smile. The tablets are still working but I wonder how much sense he is making and expect him to fall over soon.

The irrepressible lead of the movie, Tshewang Dendup, comes over and playfully drags the apple man to a huge TV screen in the corner, where a small group has gathered. The American stills photographer, Catherine Ryan, has put together a montage of behind-the-scenes photos. There are various shots of the cast and crew during takes, standing around the campfire and eating lunch. Some include the apple man. The group is delighted that he has joined them and watches for a reaction. Anything. Does he understand that's him? Has he got it yet? He remains wonderfully enigmatic, smiling at everyone, his eyes constantly twinkling, then wanders off to the buffet to help himself to some more of the wonderful food.

The apple man has no family. His wages for the film are a significant amount, more than he would earn in many years of selling apples, so Rinpoche has appointed a monk to act as an informal trustee. Karma Yangki hopes to sit next to the apple man when the finished film opens in Bhutan. She wants to see his face when he sees himself and all those days of silliness replayed up there on the big screen.

I take Kathryn off for a fresh nappy, and when we return, the room has become very quiet. It's speech time. I try to sneak back to the spot where I was sitting with the Taba girls when I recognise the voice. So does Kathryn. It's Mal. He is standing in the centre of the room bouncing on the balls of his feet, telling anecdotes about filming. He is relaxed, clever and funny. In fact he's an absolute hoot. If I didn't know he was completely off his face, I'd say he was a man in perfect control of the situation. He ends with a laugh then introduces Rinpoche.

There is a hush across the room and I can feel the crowd strain forward. Rinpoche is light, funny and clever, and says something personal about most of the crew members. There is much blushing and shuffling of feet.

Then it's over and Mal hands out certificates of appreciation signed by Rinpoche and himself to each of the 108 members of the cast and crew.

Throughout the evening Kathryn is hugged and adored by almost everyone in the room. They love her smile and red hair, and she laps up all the attention. But it finally becomes too much as she's hugged by one stranger too many and gets cranky. I retreat to a quiet spot in the hotel's reading room to feed her but can't unwrap myself enough to bare a bosom. When they dressed me in this *kira* I didn't ask how to get out of it.

A serious-looking grey-haired western man in his fifties is sitting in a leather winged armchair, reading *The Indian Times*. He glares at us when we arrive but his eyes start to sneakily check me out over the top of the paper as I struggle to get my top undone.

He offers to help. I can tell from the direction of his gaze that he doesn't mean with my crying baby. I am about to respond, not politely, when Phuntsho Wangmo appears, looking anxious. She's been searching everywhere for us. With a flick of the wrist she unfastens the elaborate gold fasteners, pulls down the top of the *kira* and I am free at last. All with complete modesty. Kathryn is instantly happy. The western man returns to his paper.

Back in the ballroom, people are starting to leave, either to go home or on to the nightclub. Some of the women change out of their *kira*s and into dancing gear – western-style tailored trousers, skirts and sequined tops, all made in India and sold in Thimphu. Wearing a belted *kira* is like being in a long corset. The fabric is so heavy and stiff that it holds everything in beautifully, but makes it impossible to wiggle those hips.

Mal is so tired that he's swaying on his feet, so we take Kathryn and head back to Taba, alone. The rest of the household isn't likely to be home for hours.

*

Mal is no help when it comes to getting out of my *kira* and I have to enlist the help of the two giggling maids. He asks me, in a slurred kind of voice, if it was a successful party and whether everybody enjoyed themselves. He remembers little of the night, and absolutely nothing of the speeches.

We are about to turn in when there's a knock at the door. It's Rinpoche with a couple of the cast and crew members in tow. He has decided that he wants to pop into the disco to say hi to everybody but he wants to go in disguise, the more outrageous the better.

While he's highly traditional, he is also known as a maverick in the world of reincarnate lamas. It is part of his style of teaching, always challenging people's paradigms, encouraging them to question their perceptions so that they will see more clearly what is real and what is their personal projection. The last place the Bhutanese would expect to see a leader of such eminent standing is in a nightclub. But why not? So that is exactly where he will go.

After much fussing and hilarity, he finally leaves Taba wearing a long dark wig, heavy black eye make-up, my Revlon 'red is red' lipstick and black western clothes. It is a cross between Japanese samurai and opera diva. He couldn't look less like a revered spiritual master.

❉

The sisters fill me in later on what happened. The disco had a long bar running along the length of a wall, a dance floor at one end of the room and two large spaces filled with groups of people drinking and yelling over the loud western rock music. There were more than 200 people crammed in there having the time of their lives. The place, according to Karma Chokyi, was jumping.

When Rinpoche arrived a frisson of excitement shot through the crowd. 'Rinpoche is here,' people whispered in wonder. Shock and surprise gave way to delight.

He only stayed about ten minutes because he doesn't enjoy smoke-filled air or thumping loud music. Nor does he drink. The stories differ, though – some people remember him being there for hours.

The wrap party and the film will be the talk of Thimphu for years, if not lifetimes, to come.

13

Leather Stew

DECEMBER 2002

With filming over and suitably celebrated, the round of dinners begins. I had thought my Taba family were the most generous, hospitable people I had ever met. I discover the whole of Bhutan is like that. And it isn't just put on for foreigners, that's how they treat each other. It seems that in rural areas, any stranger walking past any Bhutanese home would be offered food and tea.

Mal, Kathryn and I are honoured guests at a different home every night. Often when we arrive, Kathryn is whisked off us by the women of the household. It would be impolite to refuse and I realise how far I have come from those early days when I chased the Tibetan woman along the corridor of the guesthouse in Bir.

The first dinner is at the home of the police chief. He and his family live inside the heavily guarded police compound. The chief authorised four police constables to control traffic – and crowds – during the shoot and, in another peculiarly

Bhutanese gesture, has asked Rinpoche to perform a *puja* to dispel the disharmony that exists between the police and the criminals.

He invites Rinpoche and all the foreign crew to dine with his family. We make up a huge crowd of about twenty-five people sitting along the walls of two living rooms. His wife and daughters must have been at it for days, preparing the lavish buffet feast. Between courses we are entertained by a local folk band and fortified with lashings of Bhutan's fabled drink *ara*.

One of the daughters brings the *ara* around in a saucepan. It is served warm with strands of egg floating in it. She pours me a huge glass and gently warns that this drink can be an acquired taste. I'm yet to find a local brew anywhere in the world that I haven't liked and, I must say, I take to this one immediately.

Every Bhutanese household knows how to make *ara*. It is made from corn, rice or wheat, which is mixed with yeast and covered by warm blankets and plastic sheets. Folklore says that no person's shadow must fall on it while it is fermenting.

For special occasions such as this, *ara* is prepared by frying a couple of eggs in butter then adding the *ara*, allowing it to warm but not boil. Then it is served. The egg pools in the bottom of the glass and has been soaking so long that by the time I get to it, it is particularly enjoyable, like a rich liqueur.

I try to remember that I am here with Mal and Rinpoche as I happily accept my third and fourth glasses. I notice that not everyone accepts more *ara* and remind myself that I must keep myself tidy. I must, I must, I must . . . Then, just like that, it doesn't seem so important any more. Everything is amusing. These lovely people whose language I don't speak are my new best friends. And I really am the wittiest person in the world.

I'm having such a fabulous time, that when Mal retrieves Kathryn and tries to encourage me to stand up, I don't want to leave. As he physically pushes me out the door, I see the first assistant director, a likeable but rather earnest clean-cut American called Isaiah, organising the folk singers into a conga line through the police chief's living room. (The next day, as hundreds of little drums pound inside my head, I take solace from the knowledge that at least I didn't do *that*.)

❋

The following evening is dinner at the home of the King's Secretary. This is high Bhutanese cuisine and it is magnificent. Row upon row of dishes that melt in my mouth – or burn it away. There are three types of rice: red, white and brown. We wash it all down with a luscious merlot, courtesy of Taltarni Wines in Australia. For some reason that I am unable to fathom, Taltarni wines are everywhere here, served in all the best homes in Thimphu. They are the perfect accompaniment to yak.

The Secretary's home is large and very plush. We eat Bhutanese style, seated on long couches placed against the walls, with a low table in front of us. On the walls are informal photographs of the King, showing the familiar relationship this family shares with the monarch. Tonight's dinner is smaller, with Rinpoche and six or so people from the film crew and the same number from the Secretary's family, though only our host actually eats with us. The six family members stand respectfully around the table in the dining room, helping us to help ourselves to the buffet.

Here, like everywhere else we go, Kathryn is made welcome. When she isn't being cuddled and adored by the Bhutanese women, she sits wedged between Mal and me, sucking on a bottle of milk, wide-eyed and happy.

❋

The round of dinners take us inside homes all across Thimphu – from the important, influential people who have helped behind the scenes to facilitate the making of the film, and who live on the hillside overlooking the city, to the humble homes of some of the crew. One of the jolliest evenings is spent in the modest home of wardrobe assistant Ugyen Tshomo, nick-named 'Roly Poly Aunt' because of her big smile and even bigger heart.

Roly Poly Aunt has invited dozens of people to her small home on the outskirts of the city, and it's standing room only. We cram in like sardines. Making my way to the toilet involves being intimate with just about everyone along the way.

The food is simple and hearty, and I juggle it on my lap in the kitchen while sitting next to our host's sister, an amazing woman who I soon discover is a Royal Government minister. She is the Secretary to the Cabinet, one of the most influential jobs in the country. The Cabinet is currently drafting the country's first constitution.

Roly Poly Aunt's sister is in her forties, very smart and edu-cated, and keeps me enthralled as she explains the difficulties the country faces as it inches towards a democracy. No revolt-ing peasants here, ousting the royal family and chopping off their heads. The King is voluntarily relinquishing power and currently in the process of handing it over to the National Assembly.

For decades, the Dragon King, like his father before him, has been preparing the way for this bold move. The King has seen how other developing nations have moved into the modern age and doesn't want to make the same mistakes. He believes it is time for his kingdom to emerge from its isolation, but is wary of inviting the problems of the world to take root in Bhutan. In many ways the government is in an enviable position. It can look all over the world at other political and legal systems, and taking just the best, create a hybrid all its own.

Shane Simpson, Australia's top media and arts lawyer, who is doing all the legal work on *Travellers & Magicians*, has perused Bhutan's new Copyright Act. He is full of admiration for the way it has been written, describing it as 'elegant'. Compared to what he is used to – complicated, tangled laws that have been modified over the years to close loopholes and suit new conditions – Bhutan's Copyright Act is wonderfully clean.

The constitution has the potential to be just as elegant.

(Shane, who also did all the legal work on *The Cup*, tells me later that whenever he gets frustrated by a day of complicated legal problems, he opens his *Travellers & Magicians* file. The sight of the thumbprints and crosses on the Bhutanese contracts never fails to cheer him up.)

※

Another dinner is inside the royal compound of the Queens' palaces in the wealthy suburb of Motithang, high in the pine forest overlooking the city of Thimphu. Behind these same high walls, Mani Dorji's sister and her husband, who work for the royal family, have their own cottage, and it is here that Karma Yangki and Mani Dorji's three teenage daughters live.

Among the other guests are two men I recognise from the magic-school scene. They are *gomchen*, experienced meditation practitioners who were never monks but managed to pursue a spiritual life while still remaining in the secular world. They spend most of their time in their twilight years in deep and profound meditation. These *gomchen* have long grey hair, both are barrel-chested and they have an incredible aura about them. They are fabulous – powerful, relaxed, enigmatic and twinkling in the same way that the Dalai Lama seems to twinkle. I don't have to understand their language to know that they are having fun.

Both work for the royal family, performing *puja* ceremonies on auspicious dates. We all sit on comfortable rug-covered bench seats around the walls of the room, while Kathryn plays on the floor in the middle.

Our host is Gup Hopola, a smiling, gentle, humble man whose manner belies his important position. He pours us generous glasses of *ara*, with egg again, which I sip carefully, trying to avoid the floating bits. I've learned my lesson. *Caution*.

The food is laid out buffet style in a corner of the room. Pots and pots of traditional Bhutanese dishes. One dish tastes of ginger and garlic and something that I think is meat but can't be sure. It is so succulent and tender it melts in my mouth. I tell Gup Hopola how much I am enjoying it.

'Leather,' he replies.

I'm touched by his self-deprecation and seek to reassure him. 'No, no, really. It's tender and lovely,' I tell him.

He shakes his head. 'Leather,' he says again.

His wife is standing nearby, anxious that everything meets with the guests' approval. I feel embarrassed that he could make such disparaging remarks about her cooking.

'No really. I am enjoying it. It's not like leather at all.' I smile at her.

'It's leather,' he says, this time more insistent.

Mal leans over. 'It's *leather*,' he whispers. He has that look on his face that tells me he is deadly serious.

I get that feeling again, the one where I am in a play and everybody has the script but me. Karma Yangki comes to my rescue.

'It's yak hide,' she says. 'It has been boiled overnight to soften it, then stewed very slowly with ginger and garlic.' I smile back. Of course. I'm eating leather. Yak hide. How silly of me, I should have realised.

As everyone eats dinner, the conversation flows around us in Sharchop. Mal and I quietly toast the delicious leather, while Kathryn plays at our sock-covered feet.

'Do you think our shoes are okay at the front door?' I whisper. 'Mine are soft Italian leather.'

'Mmm. They would taste good with ginger and a touch of garlic,' nods Mal.

We agree that if times get really tough, we can always work our way through my shoe cupboard.

※

The next day, in the midst of the chaos that is the Prayer Flag Pictures office, Karma Yangki and I talk cooking. She gives me her recipe for riverweed soup and adds, in passing, how delicious orchids are to eat.

Karma Yangki says she knows westerners like to look at the delicate flowers and keep them in vases, but in Bhutan they are popular in salads. She tells me about a Bhutanese man married to an American woman. The wife was horrified to come home one day and find her prized orchid served to her for dinner.

And in case I ever try to recreate last night's culinary delight, she gives me some tips for cooking leather. It sparks a lively discussion among the Bhutanese, half-a-dozen of whom are crowded into the small room juggling computers on their knees, making phone calls, sorting through accounts or, like Kathryn and I, just hanging out in this lively hub.

'It's best if you get the man at the meat market to shave the hair off the yak hide,' advises Karma Yangki.

Pema Wangchuk, who runs the Siddhartha's Intent household in Delhi but has returned home to Bhutan to work as unit manager on the film, looks up from his laptop. 'Yak hide? Cow is better. It's sweeter than yak.'

'Oh no, yak hide is much tastier than cow,' Karma Yangki insists.

Phuntsho Tobgey, assistant to the producers, weighs in on the discussion. 'Cow.'

Phuntsho Wangmo hangs up the telephone and adds her ten ngultrim: 'Yak.'

'Cow.'

'Yak.'

And so it goes on.

❋

Karma Yangki's recipe for leather – yak or cow

Scrape off any remaining hair with a knife.

Soak in boiling water overnight, cleaning with water twice or more.

Boil for 1 hour in pressure cooker.

Fry with tomato, garlic and ginger in pan or pot. Add a little bit of cornflour. Add black pepper.

Serve with *ara* or a luscious Taltarni merlot.

✳

Karma Yangki's riverweed soup

Soak weed in water for 1 hour. Be vigorous to ensure all the sand is washed away.

Boil water. Add minced garlic and chopped tomato. Boil for 10 minutes.

Add weed. Boil for another 10 minutes.

Just before serving add cheese. (Karma Yangki recommends old cheese but says any cheese will do.)

14

A Very Special Lady

Mal suggests that instead of catching a plane to Delhi, we should leave Bhutan by road, and on the way to Delhi, drop in on a very special lady who lives in the Indian state of Sikkim, next door to Bhutan. We could take Kathryn to receive her blessing. It's an odd idea but intriguing. He mentions it about two weeks before we are due to go and leaves it there, just a possibility bubbling away in the background.

'Dropping in' anywhere in this part of the world is crazy enough, given the lousy roads, but expecting this most amazing woman to be home and available to see the three of us makes it one of his more impractical suggestions, I think.

Khandro Tsering Chodron is the widow of one of the greatest Tibetan masters of our times. Jamyang Khyentse Wangpo was the non-sectarian saint, scholar and principal of the renowned Dzongsar Monastery in Tibet. He himself had 113 masters and held the transmissions of all lineages of

Tibetan Buddhism, which the Bhutanese refer to as Vajrayana Buddhism.

Dzongsar Khyentse Rinpoche, Mal's 'boss', was recognised as his reincarnation at the age of seven and taken to live at the royal chapel in Sikkim, where Khandro lives. While Khandro spent her days downstairs (and still does), living a simple and devoted life of prayer, Rinpoche was schooled upstairs by his specially chosen teachers, not venturing outside until he left.

Khandro is an extraordinarily accomplished practitioner who has the respect of all in the Buddhist world. Lamas travel to Sikkim to spend time with her in her simple private room, which is dominated by a shrine to her husband, photos and an urn with some of his ashes. Her innate modesty and shyness prevent her from teaching, although she is eminently qualified to do so. As the widow of his previous incarnation, she holds a very special place for Rinpoche.

Mal has met her a few times over the years and in March 2001 I was fortunate enough to receive her blessing as part of a group of twenty taken to see her by Sogyal Rinpoche, author of *The Tibetan Book of Living and Dying* (which had been my entrée into Buddhism). It was shortly after that visit that Kathryn was conceived, which had seemed wonderfully auspicious.

A week before Kathryn's birth one of Rinpoche's students emailed us out of the blue to tell of a vivid dream she'd had of a sweet little girl dressed in white sitting with Khandro beneath the shrine to her late husband. Then Mal had walked in, which is how she knew the little girl was his daughter.

Taking Kathryn to meet Khandro and receive her blessing is a lovely, if wildly impractical, idea.

❋

Getting out of Thimphu at all turns out to be hard work.

Mal is manically trying to pay the last of the Bhutanese accounts and oversee Thimphu's largest garage sale. The production company is selling off everything, from the deep freezers to the teaspoons. A shop has been rented in the centre of town to stack it all in, floor to ceiling. Pots, pans, electrical equipment, more than a hundred mattresses, bedside lamps, wool used in the weaving scenes, eight walkie-talkies, carpet, blankets and more. Looking slightly incongruous amongst it all are two large, stainless-steel stove-top espresso makers, purchased from David Jones in Sydney and brought to Bhutan in the hand luggage of Mal's co-producer, Raymond Steiner. An Australian living in Delhi brought thirty kilos of the best coffee he could buy and what the crew haven't consumed also is for sale.

The first day of the sale is for the people who worked on the film, and the next two are for the rest of Thimphu. When the doors open, the mass of people who have been waiting pour through with unbridled glee and the same look of intensity on their faces as the bargain hunters at David Jones on Boxing Day.

The prices have been set by unit manager Pema Wangchuk. He is renowned for his good money sense and knows the financial value of every item, so can mark it down enough for it to be a bargain to the buyer without ripping off the production company. His brief is just to 'be fair'.

The sale is a huge success and the production company recoups A\$30 000.

Even the buildings that were built to house the crew are sold. One is donated to the local school in Chendebji, near the Queen Mother's yak ground where the crew lived for so many weeks. The school buys another at a reduced rate.

The rest of the buildings are sold cheaply to Trongsa Dzong, the most impressive *dzong* in the kingdom, said to be situated so high that the clouds float beneath it. It is the ancestral home of the royal family and considered to be one of the finest examples of Bhutan's distinctive architecture. Built in the 1600s, it is about to undergo a massive restoration and Prayer Flag Pictures' bamboo, wood and plastic huts will house the workers on site. They will also use the temporary underground plastic water-pipe system and electrical wiring from the camp.

The lighting and electrical equipment is sold to the Bhutanese Broadcasting Service.

At the end of the sell-off, all that is left is 18 585 metres of super 16mm film (about twenty-eight hours' worth) ready to be edited into a 108-minute movie. And Thimphu residents – arms full of second-hand homewares – have their own slice of Bhutanese film history to take home.

After the garage sale Mal and Phuntsho Wangmo are in such a state getting the locals paid, the foreigners and their equipment on planes, and all the other loose ends tied up, that our departure date changes almost by the hour. The boom operator, a fun girl from Sydney called Nicole Lazaroff, is trying to arrange to travel by road with us and, because Mal is so flat out, it is only through her that I hear the updates: we're leaving Wednesday . . . no Saturday . . . could be Sunday . . . or even Monday.

It makes no difference to me or Kathryn when we leave, which says something about how much of the relaxed Bhutanese ways I have absorbed. I think if I stayed here any longer I would probably throw away my watch altogether. The change is not lost on the family.

The sisters say we brought them an Australian baby but we are taking home a Bhutanese one. I realise how odd they found my preoccupation with putting Kathryn to bed at 7.30 every night, whether she liked it or not. Routine, I told them. They didn't get it then and they don't get it now. Nor does Kathryn. Nowadays she goes to bed either when we do or when she wants to. Somewhere along the way, without even realising it, I threw away the book.

※

Finally, one happy afternoon by the bed, while Karma Yangki is rearranging furniture and planning some major changes to her boudoir, Kathryn crawls. It is a deliriously happy moment, witnessed by most of the household.

For weeks she has been tipping forward onto her hands, into a semi-crouch, just unable to get her left leg into position. Everyone has been down on all fours showing her how, cheering her on and willing that left leg over. Three-year-old Madonna has been doing her bit by reverting to crawling in front of Kathryn.

Today, 10 December 2002, at 3.10 pm Bhutanese time, something inside her little brain clicks and, with extraordinary ease, she suddenly tips over and crawls the length of the mat. There are whoops of delight and Mal comes running in, wondering what all the noise is about. She does it again then sits on her bottom, grinning up at us all, wearing a look of complete satisfaction. I email the world with the news.

The effect this milestone has on Kathryn is remarkable. For days she beams and giggles, like she's been given the biggest boost of confidence. But being so in control now, she chooses not to repeat it for a few days. She doesn't have to. We all agree she is the cleverest baby in Thimphu.

※

Nicole gives up on us ever leaving Bhutan and makes her own arrangements. 'See you in Sydney,' she says as she waves goodbye.

She is the last of the foreign crew to go and I settle in again, no idea whether we will be driving, flying out or spending Christmas here and sending Kathryn to school down the road.

Suddenly there is a lull, and a window of opportunity opens up. Mal can leave, keeping in touch by email and phone. Everything starts to fall into place.

Rinpoche thinks it is a wonderful idea for us to visit Khandro Tsering Chodron and makes his car and driver available for the trip. Karma Loday, a cousin and frequent overnight guest of the Taba family, will drive us in the very modern and comfortable Toyota HiLux, which has air-conditioning and great suspension. He is a good driver, used to Bhutan's perilously steep and narrow roads as well as India's bumpier ones. Phuntsho Wangmo and Tenzin Wangdi need to be in Phuntsoling, so we can stay overnight with them to break up the trip.

Wesel Wangmo would like to come, to help out with Kathryn. In what seems surprising ease, everyone is able and ready to leave tomorrow. Mal phones a man in Gangtok who looks after Khandro, to see if she is home and taking visitors. He says she hasn't been well and he doesn't know whether she can see us. He will ask but won't know until we arrive.

For our final night Karma Yangki organises a special farewell dinner in the formal lounge room with all the family.

Mal and I agonise over what we can give them to thank them for their hospitality and many kindnesses. Short of leaving Kathryn with them, I can't think of anything they could possibly want.

We spend the afternoon at the biggest shop in Thimphu looking at *thangka*s, the traditional Bhutanese wall hangings of Buddhist deities. I wouldn't know a good one if I fell over it, and Mal is no better. We don't want to give something inferior – that would be so insulting. But how would we know? The family are obviously much more expert on things Bhutanese than we could ever be. We settle on two *thangka*s that the saleswoman assures us are the very best quality, and a pair of silver earrings for Wesel Wangmo as a gift from Kathryn.

In Thimphu's toy shop we find two Bhutanese Barbies, with long dark hair, dressed in *kira*s. We know they are Bhutanese because there is a large sticker that says so, obliterating the words 'Indian Barbie'. Some enterprising person buys these in India, makes up little *kira*s, and creates Bhutanese Barbies. We buy one each for Renee and Madonna.

As guests, I expected the gift-giving to be our job, but in Bhutan everybody gives. In the past week, cast and crew, some of whom I had barely spoken to, arrived at Taba with presents – cute clothes for Kathryn, a bag for me, a purse, a wooden bowl and a wall hanging.

Our Taba family present me with a stunning lavender and blue *kira* that has been made by Karma Yangki's personal weaver. It is in three pieces and they explain how it should be sewn together when I get home. They also have one for Kathryn with matching belt, *wonju* and *toego*. I recognise the bright orange stripes on the belt: Karma Yangki's mother had been weaving it on the loom in the front yard earlier in the week.

From Mani Dorji we receive a *thangka* that shows an elephant with a monkey on his back, a rabbit on the monkey's back, and a peacock on top. It is known as 'the four friends' and demonstrates working together in harmony. Everything is beautifully wrapped in the handmade paper that Bhutan is renowned for, and we open all the presents with great delight.

We hand across our presents and are anxious whether we've got it right but no-one opens our gifts, putting them aside with a thank you and a smile. I wonder if I have been gauche, ripping into my gifts like it was Christmas. The family is so understated.

They also give us a bundle of clothes for Kathryn – jumpers and pants that the girls no longer wear.

The next morning the whole family is up before dawn and stand around groggy with sleep in the driveway, ready to wish us a safe trip. There's a brief hug from each of them. No prolonged, tearful farewells here. That would imply we'd never see each other again, and may even encourage that karma. So instead, it is brief and happy, as though we are all bound to be together soon. I'm not so good at the understated and have tears in my eyes as we head off on the eight-hour drive to Phuntsoling.

※

Phuntsoling, being on the edge of the Indian plains, is much warmer and drier than the high-altitude Thimphu.

While it is on the Bhutanese side of the Indian border,

Phuntsoling is an exciting blend of the two countries. An enormous archway separates the two neighbours, and while foreigners must register, Bhutanese and Indian nationals pass freely. There are as many saris and western clothes on the streets as there are *gho*s and *kira*s.

It is lively, with an energetic buzz, and all that comes with it – lots of traffic, pollution and crime. It has none of the charm or simplicity of life in Thimphu.

It's a constant juggle for Phuntsho Wangmo and Tenzin Wangdi. Their life – family, shop and Renee's school – may be in Thimphu. But their home and the hub of the business is here in Phuntsoling.

Their home is large, comfortable and deliciously cool. They bought two adjoining apartments then knocked out a wall to create one home that seems to be a maze of rooms, winding around each other. It's a far cry from the two rooms above the shop in Thimphu.

The Phuntsoling household contains two maids and a little boy, Tshering Dorji, who turns out to be the son of the Bhutanese maid from Karma Yangki's house in Thimphu. This little boy is the result of her long and noisy labour.

The maid's pregnancy was a mystery. She wouldn't reveal who the father was and showed little interest in the boy once he was born. So, in typical Bhutanese style, the family was happy to take him in and raise him.

Tshering Dorji is a bright and cheeky little boy, who keeps Tenzin company when Phuntsho Wangmo and Renee are in Thimphu. The maids at Phuntsoling care for him when Tenzin is not around. He adores Renee when she comes to stay and the family plan that when he is old enough he will go off to school, or maybe to the monastery.

Phuntsho Wangmo is houseproud and pleased to bring out the modern crockery and dishes she has bought in Delhi. Wesel Wangmo whisks Kathryn away for some playtime and the two live-in maids serve a sumptuous feast.

I assume Wesel Wangmo eats. She appears to be a healthy

young woman. It's just that I have never seen her actually do it. Whenever food appears, she takes off with Kathryn. It makes no difference how many times I ask her to come and eat with us. She always says she has already eaten, which I'm sure can't be the case. It's like Karma Yangki always beating me to the back seat – part of their endless attempts to make life more comfortable for everybody else. Quietly, graciously and without fuss or any expectation of thanks.

The day's driving completed, Karma Loday is gone as soon as we arrive. He is a good-looking, healthy young lad and obviously has other things on his mind. Places to go, people to meet, that sort of thing. He comes in long after we've all gone to bed.

The next morning we are up early and by the time I emerge from the bathroom, Wesel Wangmo has prepared and packaged hot puréed spinach and pumpkin for Kathryn to eat along the way.

☀

We drive the three hours to Siliguri to get our visas for Sikkim. The contrast from beautiful, clean, gentle, orderly Bhutan is deafening – a cacophany of colour and movement that is any thriving Indian city. We wait in the car while Mal attends to the paperwork. The government building is teeming with people and they crowd up to the car windows, some begging, some pointing and others leering or just staring. The heat is oppressive. It is with a huge sigh of relief that we are on our way again.

It is a spectacularly beautiful journey, through the lush green rice paddies of West Bengal, then up winding forest roads that hug the cliffs. Monkeys congregate by the many bends in the roads, just where the cars have to slow down. If you slow down too much, they leap on the bonnet, cheeky and hungry.

Sikkim used to be a country of its own, another Buddhist Himalayan Shangri-la, but has since been annexed by India.

The drive is long and hot. Kathryn sleeps, then is passed around the car, from me to Wesel Wangmo, to sitting up the front on Mal's knee watching everything go by and helping change gears. Karma Loday doesn't mind. He is a capable and relaxed driver, reciting his prayers to himself under his breath as he negotiates the sharp bends.

※

We arrive at Gangtok, the hilly capital of Sikkim, and check into our hotel. Mal rings his contact, Jiga. It's good news. Khandro Tsering Chodron is home, and in good health, and we are invited for tea tomorrow morning. Meanwhile, Jiga would like us to be his guests for dinner.

Jiga is a tall handsome *khampa*, the name for the rugged men from Kham in eastern Tibet. He has high cheekbones, a ponytail and a strong presence about him. He has a wonderfully deep voice but speaks calmly and quietly.

Just after dark, he picks us up from our hotel and whisks us through back streets to his large first-floor apartment above a garage. Over dinner he talks of the forthcoming elections of the Tibetan government-in-exile. It faces many challenges, including the politicking going on among the various people standing for election. Karma Loday and Mal know the history and join in the discussion.

Part-way through the meal the lights go out. Suddenly and without warning, we are plunged into total darkness. It doesn't stop anyone for a second. The talk continues without so much as a moment's hesitation. After a few minutes of sitting and talking in total darkness, with everybody acting as if nothing has changed and this is perfectly normal, a boy emerges out of the blackness holding a gas lamp. Jiga takes it from him, still talking, and the discussion continues by gaslight.

It's a very funny scene.

'Did anyone else notice the lights go out?' I ask.

They stop momentarily and then start to laugh.

'Ha ha,' says Jiga. 'I hadn't realised how used to it we had become. It happens so often.'

※

Jiga drives us to the royal chapel, Tsuk-La-Khang, set within the grounds of the royal palace.

A group of young Indian men, who have walked up the hill to admire the view, see Kathryn on Mal's shoulders and beg for a kiss from the pretty little redhead.

I shoo them away with mock indignation and they laugh.

'We'll be back when she's older!' they call after us. Perhaps it's the altitude or the smell of juniper, but up here everybody seems light-hearted and happy.

The chapel is an impressive two-storey square building, with snow lions carved on each corner. It is set on top of a ridge with sweeping views over the valley. Old Tibetan and Sikkimese women circumambulate the walls, working their beads and saying their daily mantras. They also manage a bit of a gossip as they go. On the ledges, colourful flowers spill from old food tins. We take off our shoes at a side door and Jiga leads us through to Khandro's private room.

She is serene and beautiful, radiating calm and gentleness. Slightly stooped with grey hair, her face is unlined, and though in her seventies, she looks years younger. Khandro sits on a low bench covered in rugs, which also serves as her bed. Her hands are folded neatly in her lap, a tiny figure of self-containment.

Lining one wall are huge glass-covered bookcases filled with Tibetan texts. The only other piece of furniture is an enormous shrine that runs the length of the end wall. It has dozens of photographs, precious artefacts (some hundreds of years old) and, in a small model *stupa* in a glass case, some of her husband's ashes. She has lived and meditated in this room in front of the shrine, since he died in 1959.

Jiga introduces us and translates the pleasantries. Mal is

Rinpoche's student and they have finished shooting his new film in Bhutan, he tells her. She is interested in everything. Jiga, Wesel Wangmo, Karma Loday, Mal and I sit at her feet while Kathryn crawls up to the shrine across the clean-swept wooden floor.

'She's polishing it for you,' Mal says. Jiga translates and Khandro smiles.

She receives countless numbers of visitors from all over the world who come, like us, just to be in her presence. She treats everyone with such grace, as if each one is special to her.

After inspecting the shrine, Kathryn crawls over to Khandro and sits contentedly near her feet. Khandro gives her blessing, patting her on the head.

We stay for half an hour then are led by an elderly monk, who looks after Khandro, into another room for tea, served in dainty china cups, and sweet biscuits. It is another simply furnished room, with low benches covered in Tibetan rugs. This is where the monk lives.

After our visit we feel buoyant. Leaving the chapel grounds, the sun is shining over the valley, and young monks are washing their clothes in a quadrangle.

We spend a lazy afternoon and evening in Gangtok then head off early the next morning to fly to Delhi. Karma Loday drops us off at Bagdogra Airport before he and Wesel Wangmo start the long drive back to Bhutan. She holds Kathryn close to her for one final hug. Clearly it is a wrench to say goodbye.

Bagdogra is a military airport with fierce security and lots of loud, bad-tempered Indians. Standing in the queue at check-in a middle-aged Indian man in a grey suit rams his trolley into the back of my legs to get in front of me. I have Kathryn in my arms and we both nearly tumble over as my knees start to buckle.

'Careful . . . my baby,' I mumble, stunned at his rudeness.

He won't meet my eye, just manoeuvres his trolley around me, going for the gap.

It's a shock to be back in India.

※

There is no space in Mal's small room in Delhi to set up Kathryn's cot so she sleeps on a blanket in the suitcase by the bed. She's become used to sudden changes in her surroundings and is oblivious to the constantly ringing phones and the comings and goings of the Siddhartha's Intent household.

Before returning to Australia, Mal needs to check on the buildings in Bir so after a few days, we catch the overnight train to Pathankot. It has to be one of the most enjoyable ways to spend a night, gently rocked to sleep by the train's motion.

We arrive at 6 am and Ugyen Thrinley, one of Rinpoche's monks from Bir, is there to meet us at the station. He is delighted to see Kathryn again and immediately takes her from my arms. It is too early for any shops to be open so we drive for a few hours to a small cafe by the roadside that serves wonderful pickled mushroom omelettes.

It is a popular spot, below a nunnery and overlooking a waterfall that flows over huge boulders. Everywhere are wild monkeys. Many boulders on the Indian roads are painted with advertisements, usually for school supplies and IT courses. Here we see a rock, halfway up, with the word 'Bunty', painted in red lettering.

My real name is Carolyn, and 'Bunty' is an affectionate nickname given me by my English father that the whole family came to use. When the children at school teased me about it, and I wanted to revert to Carolyn, he assured me it was common in England. I lived in London for three years and found no such thing. Perhaps it was common fifty years ago but the English people I met thought it must be a peculiar Australianism. Strangely enough, here in India it turns out to be quite common. There is even a chain of stationery shops called Bunty's Supplies.

While we eat our pickled mushroom omelettes and watch monkeys climb all over the Bunty rock, two busloads of Indians arrive. There are about sixty women, men and children and they swarm into the cafe. One woman spots Kathryn and rushes over, followed by another, and another. They remark on her hair. They have never seen anything like it and ask if they can touch it.

They are very friendly and explain that they are from one large extended family and have rented two buses for a fortnight's holiday.

One asks if she can be photographed with our beautiful baby. Kathryn seems happy enough with all the attention so we hand her over. The woman cradles her in her arms and Kathryn smiles on cue. Two more women ask if they can pose with her. We happily oblige. Other members of the family see what is going on and rush over. It starts a mini stampede and we are horrified as we lose sight of our little baby. We are jostled out of the way as more cameras are produced and the family starts to hand her around. I'm sure they don't mean to be unkind or insensitive but I can hear Kathryn start to cry, and I panic.

'Give me back my baby!' I scream, pushing through the crush of bodies. For one long, anxious moment it is chaos as I fight my way to her. Some of the family stand back in shock, while a couple of women see instantly what has happened and rush to help.

The woman holding her is trying to soothe her while still smiling for the camera.

'Give her back,' I demand.

'But I haven't had my photo taken,' she wails.

'Give me back my baby,' I hiss. 'GIVE HER TO ME!'

She looks startled and reluctantly passes me Kathryn, who is by now hysterical.

I flash the most evil look I can manage and return with my sobbing baby to Mal and Ugyen Thrinley.

Get me to Bir.

*

The first of a new set of buildings that Mal was designing on our last visit is finished and Rinpoche's household of monks have moved in.

It is wonderful, with a fabulous view over the Kangra Valley. We can watch the evening entertainment, that glorious blood-red sunset, from the verandah outside our room on the first floor.

It's far enough away from the main road that we don't hear the thundering tractor trolleys or the incessant blasting of horns. Even the barking dogs seldom bother to come down here. The only sounds are the birds, chanting monks – and Kathryn.

Unfortunately, surrounded by all this serenity, when she lets loose she sounds loud, very loud. I feel guilty for the monks in their meditations. Her bath is the kitchen sink and her playpen, our bed.

We have no toys, but I doubt Kathryn notices. She is happy playing with her own box of goodies – a thermos lid, two limes, a bunch of keys, an empty toilet roll and a small tin of lip salve. They keep her entertained for hours.

The three of us spend most of the day on the bed, Mal and I working on our laptops, while Kathryn rolls the limes around in the thermos lid. We meet up with the rest of the household for meals.

Some of the monks who live here work each day typing precious Buddhist texts into computers to eventually be published on CD-ROMs.

When China invaded Tibet and destroyed monasteries many precious Buddhist texts were lost forever. Rinpoche, along with other lamas, is committed to preserving the ancient Buddhist texts that did make it out of Tibet, as well as translating them for westerners. Tucked away in this quiet little corner, adrift from most mod cons, it is not uncommon to see monks in their robes, walking around with a laptop under their arm.

Christmas Day passes like any other day. Being surrounded

by Buddhist Tibetans who are surrounded by Hindu Indians, we are a long way from Christian celebrations in the larger cities. The view of snow-capped mountains from our window is, however, just like a Christmas card.

Many of the monks in Rinpoche's household are Bhutanese, and the food, prepared by a monk and the resident Indian cook, is reminiscent of Karma Yangki's home.

Lots of chilli, cheese, meat and vegetables. It is always fresh, tasty and plentiful.

On Christmas Day, by chance, the monk, Ridzin Dorji, produces one of his most brilliant culinary feats – a burnt chilli sauce. He serves it with boiled meat but says it goes just as well with pasta. As with Karma Yangki, he doesn't know quantities, cooking with instinct and lots of tasting along the way.

※

Khyentse chilli sauce

Brown large red chillies in a saucepan over a flame till almost, but not quite, burnt.
Mix in a small saucepan with tomatoes, cheese, salt, onion, coriander and milk powder.
Sensational!

※

After ten days Mal has talked at length with the Tibetan overseer and given plans for the next stage of building to Ugyen Thrinley. It's time to go home. Mal's due to meet the film editors, I've got to meet book editors, and Kathryn – well she's about due for some warm weather. We land in Sydney just as the 9 pm fireworks explode over the harbour heralding the end of 2002.

15

Back for More Yak

AUGUST 2003

Mal's movie has undergone eight months of intensive post-production in Sydney, my book is at the typesetters, and Kathryn has blossomed into a walking, talking toddler.

It has been an exhausting period, with both of us working from home under pressure to meet our respective deadlines, while juggling Kathryn between us. Our lounge room, which doubles as Mal's production office, has been dominated by his huge desk overflowing with papers, and the telephone has been ringing day and night with calls from America, London and Bhutan. Because of the time difference with the other countries, Mal's day would end at around two or three in the morning, a few hours before Kathryn and I would wake. For months we lived our life in shifts and I dearly missed the relaxed pace of the house in Taba.

So it is with great excitement that we fly back to Bhutan for the world premiere of *Travellers & Magicians*. This time I know what to expect and I'm almost delirious with anticipation.

I can't wait to see the family and for them to see Kathryn, with all her new-found abilities.

✳

While Mal sorts out the complicated visas and associated paperwork inside the terminal at Paro International Airport, I change Kathryn's nappy and she says, 'Walk.' It's not a request but, like everything else these days, a demand.

Nearly eighteen months old, she has entered her wilful stage, as the book so fondly refers to it. She wants to walk through customs just like everyone else. And why not? I pop her down on her feet but every few steps, she falls over. Being so independent she hates holding our hands, so we know she is having serious trouble on her own when she allows us to take a hand each. Then she's fine. As soon as she gets her confidence back, she lets go of our hands.

'Walk,' she declares and strides forward, only to fall flat on her face.

She is more indignant than hurt. And shocked. She had this walking thing figured out so she can't make sense of why the ground keeps coming up to greet her. Mal and I think we may have an idea why. Rubber legs. We know that feeling. We have it after too much wine or *ara* or whatever. In her case, she's still drugged.

We grimace at each other and feel a twinge of guilt. Phenurgen. It's an antihistamine meant for allergies. One of the side effects for babies is that it puts them to sleep, and while no-one would actually prescribe it, from the moment she was born, people have mentioned it to us in a conspiratorial whisper. One woman who travelled on her own with three children to New York once asked if Kathryn had met 'Finnigan' yet. That was her code name for the wonder drug. We gave Kathryn a small dose after leaving Bangkok and she slept all the way through the stopovers in Rangoon and Dacca, waking up just as the pilot dropped the wheels to land at Paro.

Maybe we overdid the dose? She looks chirpy but it can't be good that her legs aren't working.

It's only when I hoist her up that I realise she has both legs through one leg of her shorts. In my jet-lagged state, when I changed her nappy I put both legs through by mistake. I may as well have tied her knees together. Poor little thing. No wonder she keeps falling over.

I strip her down by the luggage carousel and dress her properly. She is delighted. Everything works again. And so she strides through customs into Bhutan.

☀

Waiting by his car outside the airport doors is Karma Loday with a welcoming smile on his face. We've been invited to a picnic, he tells us cheerfully.

He drives us to a glorious spot by the river where Rinpoche is enjoying lunch and we recognise a few faces from the post-film round of dinners. The Chief of Police is here as is the wife of the King's Secretary. And the young man who sat behind us on the plane. I eavesdropped on his conversation all the way so already I know a lot about him. He was studying IT in Ontario, Canada and was seated on the plane next to a couple who were returning to Bhutan after two years, studying IT in Melbourne. I know how much they each expect to earn, how many Bhutanese there were in Melbourne (about forty) and how they thought the Australian accent was so odd. 'Gidday maaate' and 'Roight' they said to each other and laughed.

This couple are among the eighty-seven Bhutanese students currently studying in Australia, thirty-two of them on AusAID scholarships. It's part of an ongoing arrangement between the two countries that started in the 1960s. Formal diplomatic relations were established in September 2002, and in May 2003, when Australia's first ambassador to Bhutan, Penelope Wensley, was 'presenting her credentials to His Majesty the King', she promised that as part of the next stage, the Federal

Government wanted to help Bhutan establish a university. Other countries are just as keen to offer places at university for young Bhutanese and it is lovely to hear this man's impressions of his time in Canada.

The Bhutanese set a new standard for picnics. It is monsoon season so everything is lush and the river is full and gushing. Woollen rugs and bamboo mats are laid out under the shade of a huge tree and hot dishes lined up in heatproof containers. Meat *momos*, cheese *momos*, buckwheat noodles and pancakes, *emmadatshi*, beans, boiled meat and the biggest treat of all – Buddha mushrooms, which grow wild in Bhutan and have just come into season. Known as masutaki mushrooms in Japan, and costing around US$2000 a kilo, they are a delicacy appreciated all over the world. They taste similar to the shiitake but more buttery.

It is a wonderful way to re-enter the country. The setting and the summer day are sublime.

Mal and Rinpoche talk film business. *Travellers & Magicians* has just been invited to screen at the prestigious Venice Film Festival, alongside movies by Woody Allen, Bernardo Bertolucci, Ridley Scott, the Coen brothers and Lars Von Triers. This is an accolade in itself and it has generated much excitement in film circles. They couldn't have planned a better way to launch the film on the world.

✳

After lunch we drive to Thimphu, along the twisted mountain roads that run beside the flowing river. By the roadside are occasional stalls with locals in the traditional *kira* or *gho*, selling bunches of wild asparagus. There are temples on just about every hill and road pass, surrounded by tall, erect prayer flags fluttering in the breeze.

The drive is so long because the road is narrow and winding, and our speed seldom rises over thirty kilometres an hour. Indian-made four-wheel drive vehicles take up most of the road, so it takes some effort to get past. There are many heart-stopping moments looking down the sheer slope to the raging rivers below. Fortunately the drivers defer to each other and there is no aggressive posturing over who goes first.

Our first stop is at the Royal Institute of Management on the outskirts of the capital, where tomorrow the film will have its royal premiere. It's going to be a huge event with all four Queens of Bhutan in attendance. Phuntsho Wangmo has been working day and night to make sure everything is just right.

Thimphu's two cinemas are not considered glamorous enough to host such an auspicious event so the main hall of the school has been chosen. They have had to bring in a screen and projector, and lengths of white cloth to cover the seats to make them worthy of a royal behind. While helpers drape the seats, the tech people are doing a run-through to check the sound levels.

The hall is dark but, as we stand in the doorway looking in, there is a cry of recognition. Karma Yangki and Phuntsho Wangmo rush over and it's hugs and kisses all round, with much cooing over Kathryn. Just about everybody I met in Bhutan is here, sitting in the dark, dying for a glimpse of the much-awaited movie, and we are suddenly surrounded by familiar faces.

Mal wanders off, deep in discussion with the technicians. It's news to me, but there are different *grades* of screen – some are whiter than others, some more even, and it all makes a big difference to the enjoyment of the film. This one has a crease in it which is causing concern. Also, they need to make a decision about how to frame it on the screen. Should there be space below the subtitles, or should they rest right on the lower edge?

Kathryn greets each person who comes up to her with a shy 'hi', and a little wave. They can't believe how much she has grown. Karma Chokyi is here but youngest sister Wesel Wangmo has gone to India to study. This is enrolment weekend and she can't leave. Karma Chokyi says she was very disappointed to miss seeing Kathryn.

In the front row is a smiling face I recognise but can't quite place. After a few minutes I remember. It's the apple man! Neatly shaven and wearing a toothless grin from ear to ear, he is sitting in the middle of this mayhem, happily watching it all go on around him. I don't believe he could possibly remember me, having met for just two minutes at the wrap party eight months ago, but he spots me and waves. I'm sure he's just getting into the spirit of it all.

He seems altogether different from before. He isn't a big man but when he stands up he seems taller than I remember. And that smile just doesn't leave his face.

'What's with the apple man?' I ask.

It turns out that about three months ago he at last discovered that he'd been involved in making a film. All the mad behaviour by the roadside with Rinpoche and that bunch of crazy foreigners suddenly made sense, and ever since he's been telling anybody who will listen: 'I'm in a movie.' The transformation is remarkable. Instead of a rabbit caught in the headlights, he now looks more like the cat that got the cream. Clearly he's having the time of his life.

*

Finally, towards the end of the afternoon, we head off to Taba, bypassing the centre of town, taking the winding road past the magnificent building of Trashi Chhoe Dzong, with its distinctive yellow roof and golden spires. The air is fresh and alive with birds. It is glorious.

We find the Taba house has changed dramatically in the past eight months. Like most things Bhutanese, it is fluid and dynamic, changing to suit the family's needs. Walls have been knocked down and new ones erected. They didn't go to the council to get approval, they didn't even draw up plans. Karma Yangki just got the builders in and told them what she wanted, and they did it.

What was her bedroom is now like a small apartment in the

middle of the house, with an en-suite bathroom and a bedroom for Madonna and Karma Chokyi. The wall beside the bed was knocked out to create a larger living area. It is where the family spends most of their time so it makes sense. Instead of just a mat in the small space by the bed, where Kathryn crawled for the first time, now there is a lounge suite and a low coffee table. A new wall divides the downstairs lounge room, creating a hallway-cum-room where the fridge now grandly resides. The kitchen has been moved to the outhouse that used to be the weaving room.

Most dramatic of all is an enormous new waterbed in the centre of the room. It is huge. Unfortunately, after they bought the waterbed Mani Dorji discovered he couldn't sleep on it because it made him feel seasick, so he and Karma Yangki now have another, newly created bedroom. They live, entertain and relax here, but sleep elsewhere. The waterbed has become a play pen, the family's favourite spot for watching TV.

Madonna and Renee are excited to see Kathryn and race up to greet us. She waddles up and pokes at them, which terrifies them anew. She has doubled in size and now moves and talks – not what they remember of the little person who sat in one spot and giggled. The little girls retreat behind the maid's skirt and stay there, peeking out, unsure quite what to make of her.

It has taken days of travelling to get here and Mal, Kathryn and I are exhausted. After hot sweet tea, we collapse on our bed upstairs just as the afternoon's monsoon storm begins. The rain pounds on the tin roof and the upstairs kitten curls up with the three of us for a late afternoon nap.

Mal sleeps for hours but Kathryn is too excited by all the smells and noises of her new surroundings to stay down for long, so we go visiting.

It's all happening around the waterbed. Mani Dorji is sitting on the floor watching a Hindi movie on TV. A little terrier dog is chasing the downstairs kitten and they keep streaking through the room, then stopping to wrestle on the floor. Karma Chokyi is on the couch watching Karma Yangki, who is trying on various *kira*s, holding them up for everybody's verdict. She has had one woven especially for tomorrow's royal occasion but still isn't sure it is suitable. Most of the Taba family are acting as ushers to members of the royal family, escorting each one individually to their seats, so it is vitally important that they look their best. Kathryn is delighted to spot a telephone, just like at home, and waddles over to poke at it.

Phuntsho Wangmo's husband Tenzin has just returned from a tour of America with three others from Bhutan's business community. They were sent by the government to observe how small businesses are encouraged and supported in America. He says he was surprised by the degree of corporate help. Compared to Bhutan, where the government is involved in everything, America's small businesses rely heavily on the support of their own business community. He has come back full of ideas of how to help fledgling businesses in his own country. He admits he only just made it back in time for tomorrow's gala event.

I ask about the little boy he looks after in Phuntsoling. Tenzin tells me that the boy's mother, one of the Taba maids during my previous stay, has taken him and they have started a new life together in a country village. Everyone is happy at how it turned out.

The new maid, a young girl who must be about thirteen (but no-one seems to know), brings us tea by the bed. She is very petite, only coming up to my waist, and sweet. Kathryn keeps pointing to her and saying, 'Baby.'

❋

The next morning the sisters dress me in my own beautiful lavender-coloured *kira* and matching belt – their farewell gift to me in December. In Sydney I had the three lengths of woven fabric sewn together as the sisters had suggested, and according to the precise instructions of a Bhutanese girl whose husband is studying agriculture at the University of Sydney. She explained where each piece should be sewn and how the rough edges should be trimmed. I found a local dressmaker to do the job.

Determined not to look so clumsy this time, I have brought high-heel sandals and jewellery to match. Karma Yangki completes the ensemble with a *wonju*, a *toego* and two elaborate gold brooches (*komas*) that fasten the *kira* at the shoulders. Karma Chokyi pulls the belt in so much I feel like Scarlett O'Hara in *Gone with the Wind*. Seeing the look of pain on my face, she asks if it's too tight.

'How tight would you wear it?' I ask.

She pulls the belt in even more.

I gasp. 'Okay.'

'Are you sure? We Bhutanese women are used to it.'

'Then I'll get used to it,' I say through gritted teeth.

It's Kathryn's turn next and she fights us every step of the way. We give up on trying to get the shirt onto her, and it takes two of us to hold the wriggling mass while Karma Chokyi fastens her little *kira* at the shoulders with safety pins. We tie a matching belt around her waist and over the top goes a vivid orange *toego*. To complete her ensemble, she wears hot-pink patent leather shoes. She looks adorable. Grumpy, but gorgeous. She recovers swiftly from the indignity of it all and chases after the little white terrier.

Mal takes us on a bumpy ride along potholed roads over-grown with marijuana bushes, past the National Mushroom Centre and through an ornate ceremonial archway to the Royal Institute of Management. 'Welcome to the world premiere of *Travellers & Magicians*,' proclaims a hand-painted sign in gold lettering.

The film is multi-layered, featuring a story within a story, and so too are the premieres – all three of them. First up this Saturday afternoon is the royal premiere, attended by the pinnacle of Bhutanese society.

The cast arrives first, and are talked through their roles for the afternoon. They assemble on the red carpet next to Rinpoche and Mal, ready to greet the VIPs. Most of the crew is here also, to watch and help in any way they might be needed. The talent co-ordinator, Chooing, the lovely young woman who collects other people's garbage on the weekends, comes up and straightens Kathryn's *kira*. She whips off the safety pins at her little shoulders and produces two dress pins. Amazingly, Kathryn doesn't struggle. 'Much more elegant,' she declares when she's finished.

Kathryn and I find a spot on the top floor, overlooking the entrance, where we can see everything that is going on and Kathryn's cries of 'Daddy, Daddy' won't distract anyone.

First come the *gomchen*. Their long grey hair is tied back in neat buns and they wear robes with long shawls draped over one shoulder. The picture of dignity, they smile as they walk up the carpet, greeting Rinpoche, the cast and Mal, then melt into the crowd inside.

The sun is shining but the air is heavy with moisture as monsoon clouds gather for the late afternoon downpour. The imminent arrival of the regal party is heralded by a posse of fit, athletic young military men in blue paratrooper suits who do a reconnaissance of the building.

A few minutes later a hush descends and everyone looks at their feet. The black royal Land Cruisers have arrived. For the members of the cast, lined up to greet the royal entourage, today is a rare opportunity to actually look their first family in the eye, as protocol normally forbids it.

The Queens are resplendent in beautifully coloured silk *kira*s. It is an unusual event for all four sisters, and their children, to be in attendance. Only the King and Crown Prince are absent, busy seeing to urgent matters of state. The Dragon King will watch a video in the privacy of his palace later.

The rest of his family strolls up the red carpet, a huge smiling party of twenty-four. Kathryn and I watch as the ushers (including Karma Yangki, Mani Dorji, Phuntsho Wangmo and Tenzin Wangdi) each escorts a royal to their seat. Even though this movie is the biggest cultural event to hit the nation in a decade or more, and this screening the most prestigious, inside the hall there are many empty seats. It just wouldn't be right to 'crowd' the royals.

As the film unfolds, the room is conspicuously quiet. No subject would dare laugh or even breathe too loudly for fear of distracting the royals. Again, I find myself astonished at the degree of respect and devotion the Bhutanese feel for their first family.

For the 108 minutes that the film plays, Kathryn and I sit in the shade, walk around the grounds and try to stay cool. The grey clouds look ominous, preparing for the afternoon onslaught, and the humidity is rapidly rising. I feel trapped inside all these layers of fabric but dare not undo anything, knowing I will never get it back together again.

I have some vague idea that I might get Kathryn to sleep in the car, but she is much too stimulated by all the excitement to co-operate. When the film finishes and the audience comes out of the theatre we stand off to one side, trying to keep out of the way. It's useless. Kathryn spots Mal's head above the crowd, screams 'Daddy' and pushes through everybody to get to him. Then she wraps herself around his legs with delight, as if she hasn't seen him for a month.

Afterwards, while monsoon rain pounds the roof, a genteel reception is held in a massive marquee in the institute's grassy courtyard. The marquee is white, decorated with fierce dragons clutching jewels in their talons. Above the courtyard the cast and other guests stand in the hallway and watch through windows, while inside the marquee two rows of sofas covered in rugs have been placed looking outwards. The four Queens, Princes, Princesses, Rinpoche and another lama, Rabjam Rinpoche, sit in the front row. Behind them in the second row sit Mal, Kathryn and I with the King's Secretary. It's cooler in here and I feel elegant and demure in my *kira*, arranging it carefully around my feet just like the royal ladies. One Queen turns and chats to us as waiters bring orange juice in long-stemmed glasses and a selection of hors d'oeuvres.

Kathryn is unable to sit still and runs out onto the grass to play in the rain. The Queens appear to be enchanted by this little redhead in a *kira* frolicking in front of them like some sort of floorshow. I'm aghast. I'm not well versed in Bhutanese royal protocol but suspect this isn't quite the done thing. I pray she will come back inside the marquee on her own but, of course, she doesn't, and I have to go out in the rain to get her. She thinks it's a huge game and I give up kidding myself that I look elegant as I hitch up my *kira* and in front of the royal party chase after her in high heels across the muddy grass.

The Queens smile sympathetically. Maybe royal toddlers are just as badly behaved.

I try taking her hand to lead her gently back inside the tent. 'No!' she says, shaking me off, stamping her foot and running away. I laugh merrily. She never does this at home, I say to anyone who can hear. Can't think what's got into her . . . I keep smiling.

She runs off again. I finally catch her, pick her up and drag her kicking and screaming into a corner of the tent, as far away from the Queens as I can get. Bad move. There is a TV set up to play excerpts from the movie. It is plugged in and ready to go, just needing someone to press the on switch. It's a Sony, almost identical to the one in our lounge room in Sydney. The way Kathryn sees it, that switch is all that stands between her and Bob the Builder. So she presses it, then keeps hitting buttons. One of them is for volume. At eighteen months, she knows exactly what she is not supposed to do and delights in doing it. Every time. As she holds her finger on the button, the sound of static gets louder and louder, filling the tent like 1000 snakes have been unleashed in the corner. Heads start to swivel. In the time it takes me to throw myself on Kathryn and hit the off button, all the Princesses have stopped talking among themselves and are staring straight at us.

Kathryn is so overtired from all the excitement and lack of an afternoon nap that any kind of control is virtually impossible. But I fear that leaving before the Royals would be a gross breach of etiquette. Smiling gaily, I shepherd her into a back corner of the marquee and for the next half-hour sit on the floor and roll walnuts across the carpet to her.

At 6 o'clock on the dot, the four Queens rise to leave. One Queen shakes my hand and says how much she enjoyed meeting our beautiful little girl, which is very kind but not entirely believable. Another tells Mal how much she enjoyed the film. It's hard to imagine these elegant ladies, with their gracious manners and serene smiles, ever uttering anything negative or derogatory. Nevertheless, they have given the film the all-important royal nod and everyone is pleased.

As the Queens and their entourage walk along the halls of the school, the crowd parts, then closes again behind them. The Royals stop at each cast member to compliment them on their performances. When they get to the apple man I think he may just burst with pride. I swear he has grown another inch since yesterday.

✳

In the evening, Rinpoche is having dinner inside the royal compound and we are invited.

The collection of palaces is high on the hillside and as Mal pushes Phuntsho Wangmo's little Maruti up the steep incline, it starts to splutter and make hissing noises. There is a loud plop and steam gushes out of the bonnet and covers the wind-screen. We've blown a hose. Mal telephones our host from a shop nearby, explains the problem, and within minutes Tenzin Wangdi appears. No problem, he says, he will come back for the car in the morning.

The home is the same one where we enjoyed leather stew on our previous visit. This evening our host is not the head of the household, Gup Hopola, but one of the *gomchen*, who works with the royal family. The doctor from the Dzongkha Com-mittee, Pema Dorji, who attended Mal when he was sick with sinusitis, is also invited. Everyone is in high spirits after the successful royal premiere and while Karma Yangki keeps filling our glasses with more *ara*, the conversation flows around us in Sharchop, fast and furious.

The men are all obviously old friends and there is much teasing of the doctor, a renowned ladies' man. There is a bit of banter between them, then they all fall about laughing. Rinpoche translates some of what is being said, but is laughing too much to reveal all. After dinner the men settle into a game of cards and we take Kathryn home.

As we park the car in the driveway a familiar face opens my door. It's Wesel Wangmo. She has travelled by train and bus to get here, telling her bemused teachers that she just has to go home for a day or two. Kathryn is sound asleep in my arms and Wesel tenderly strokes her face, marvelling at how much bigger she is. Kathryn doesn't stir. Their reunion will have to wait till morning.

❋

Over sweet tea by the waterbed, the sisters swap notes on the afternoon. None of them actually saw the film, they were so busy organising it all. They are tired but elated. They laugh at one non-Bhutanese guest who was introduced to one of the Queens. In response to the polite royal query 'How are you?', the foreigner replied that she was well and then asked after the Queen's health. The sisters look knowingly at each other.

I don't understand. They explain that it's a breach of protocol to ask a royal a question. You answer them, but you certainly don't ask them. It doesn't matter though, they rush to explain. Being a foreigner and unused to Bhutanese ways, it was an entirely forgivable faux pas.

Lordy, lordy – *now* they tell me.

I try to repeat to them every polite pleasantry I think I might have exchanged with Their Royal Highnesses. It was small talk, either about Kathryn or the film, but I can't guarantee I didn't ask anything. I was so concerned with keeping my wayward daughter in check that I don't actually remember.

They assure me I shouldn't worry. The Queens wouldn't be offended, they say.

※

The following afternoon is premiere number two – government ministers and VIPs of Thimphu. The National Assembly is meeting on Monday so all the ministers are here, and on every seat is a VIP bottom.

Travellers & Magicians is shot in Dzongkha, but as only a quarter of the country speaks it, the film is shown with English subtitles.

Dzongkha is a complex language and many Bhutanese videos portray it badly, mixing it with modern idiom, and even though foreigners won't notice, it is a matter of national pride that *Travellers & Magicians* gets it right. This audience of scholars, senior bureaucrats and ministers will be the harshest critics.

After the screening there is much discussion about what aspects of Bhutan the film will present to the world at large, but on one thing the men seem to agree: the Dzongkha is concise and accurate. The big boys give it the nod.

The final premiere, in the evening, is for the teachers and students of the Royal Institute of Management, as a thank you for providing the venue. They crowd into the hall, spilling out of seats and onto the floor, full of enthusiasm and curiosity.

Thimphu has a video hall that shows Bhutanese videos, and an old-style cinema (the Lugor) that shows mainly Hindi movies or the occasional Hollywood blockbuster. This group are the most frequent patrons of both, and are familiar with the language of cinema. They represent the modern face of Bhutan.

The students laugh loudly and lustily, completely captivated by the story and the characters. It is a huge hit and they leave on a high, discussing with relish the nuances and layers of meaning. Many say they want to see it again, immediately.

In just two days, *Travellers & Magicians* has been seen, approved and appreciated by a cross-section of Bhutanese. It will now open in Thimphu's two cinemas and by the end of its two-week run, most of the 47 000 residents should have seen it at least once.

⁕

Monday morning is hectic again for Phuntsho Wangmo. Mal is chasing her to sit down and do accounts, and I want to get her alone for a private chat, but she has the rest of the week's screenings to organise so neither of us has much luck. All of Thimphu want to be among the first to see the film and tickets are sold out. In such a close-knit community, everybody is connected and she's feeling the pressure of people asking for favours.

Kathryn and I head home in a taxi with Wesel Wangmo. She tells me she has to leave on the bus tomorrow, to get back to school. It was a lot of travelling for such a short visit but she says it was worth it to see Kathryn.

Back at Taba, I finally get the chance to catch up with Karma Chokyi. I am dying to know how her exams went and, most importantly, how the love affair with Dr Thinley Norbu is progressing. We sprawl across Karma Yangki's waterbed and settle in for a catch-up.

The exams were okay, she says, and after they finished, she and her cousin Karma Yogini went back to the village for their much-anticipated holiday to visit their grandmother. They had a wonderful time and, best of all, she found a piece of paper that showed when each family member was born. She *is* twenty-six years old, born in the Year of the Snake, she tells me proudly. There is enough information for her sister Pema Bidha (the one studying astrology in India) to do her chart.

After the holiday she took a short-term job with the government doing survey work, which took her all over the countryside interviewing people in their homes. One of the places she and the rest of her team stayed was near the clinic where Dr Thinley is now working.

They spent a little time together but, she says with a grimace, the romance has petered out. She shrugs: 'I don't think he is the one.'

Part of the problem seems to be his attitude to her working outside the home once they were married. He indicated that he would prefer she didn't work, and that worried her. But also, most telling of all, he just didn't make her heart beat faster.

Karma Chokyi wonders where she will meet new prospects, living here with her sisters. But she's not concerned enough to settle for something that isn't quite right. Instead she is looking to her career and plans to take another job doing survey work.

✳

It takes just a day for the girls to feel comfortable with Kathryn, and she to get used to her new surroundings again. Her body clock is on Sydney time so she wakes before dawn, ready to play with Madonna and Renee. Unfortunately, like the rest of the house, they are asleep.

The stairs are steep and we all worry that Kathryn will fall down them. But she is determined and if we lose sight of her for a minute, we always know exactly where to look. The stairs. Inevitably she will be sitting on the top one, looking down, thinking, thinking. When her confidence is up, she very carefully lowers her bottom over the edge of one, then the next one. Within a few days she has them conquered and spends most of her time upstairs trying to go downstairs to find the girls.

✳

In the evening, Mal and I are served dinner in the upstairs dining area. One by one, everyone wanders up until it becomes

215

an impromptu family dinner party. Karma Yangki and Phuntsho Wangmo sit with us at the table while their two little girls play chasey with Kathryn. Karma Chokyi brings out a bottle of French red wine, which only she and I drink. Karma Loday drops by and eats standing against a wall. Wesel Wangmo doesn't eat but positions herself on the floor at the top of the stairs to stop Kathryn in case she falls down.

Mal and I brought presents for the girls and this seems the perfect time to give them. A new outfit for their Barbie dolls, a little purse with kiddie make-up and a top each, which we hope four- and five-year-old girls will think is pretty groovy. The make-up purses – each with a little mobile phone on a keyring containing a rainbow of eye shadows – are a big hit and the girls spend the rest of the evening inspecting each item, then putting them back in the purses, only to take them out again a few minutes later.

After dinner I corner Phuntsho Wangmo and make her sit down in the lounge room with a cup of tea and a printout of my book so far. It is the beginning of a very scary few hours. When this family opened their doors to Kathryn and I, they had no idea that I was a writer or that I intended to write about their lives. And, at the time, I had no such intentions.

When I did start writing this book, it was always with the idea that I would show the family first. If they didn't like it, it was going in the bin. It's one thing to live with a family, sharing all their intimacies, quite another to write it up for all the world to read.

What if they were offended by my view of their lives? Insulted even? What if I had got some of it horribly wrong? How would I feel if the situation were reversed and someone I had given hospitality to repaid the favour by exposing my daily life and what I kept in my fridge? Not that putting myself in their shoes is necessarily much help. Their customs are so complicated and different from mine that the potential for blunder is enormous.

Phuntsho Wangmo is senior enough in the family to speak

for everybody and is the most fluent in English. I figure she is the best starting point.

She sits down on a couch and, with Renee on her lap and Kathryn climbing on top of them both, starts to read. The rest of the family has retired downstairs for the night and Mal is working away on his laptop on a couch opposite.

Phuntsho Wangmo is slow and meticulous, reading every word with a slight frown. Barely five minutes into it, she stops and points out an ambiguity. In describing the Taba household I have mentioned three sisters and one husband. It makes it sound like all three sisters are married to Mani Dorji, she says. That hadn't occurred to me. But in this country, where multiple marriages are common, it leaps off the page at her. I give her a red pen and she makes a correction. Without another word, she resumes reading.

My heart sinks. I feel nauseous. Mal looks up every now and then and gives me a sympathetic look. He understands how nerve-racking this is.

The two girls are playing with Renee's make-up purse and the room is quiet, except for Mal's typing and Phuntsho Wangmo turning a page every minute or so.

I pretend to write emails but, over the top of the screen, I'm watching her reading my take on life with her family.

She gets to the pages describing the first week where Kathryn cried so much and I was nearly demented with no sleep. She makes a clucking sound with her tongue. 'We didn't realise Kathryn cried so much at night,' she says, shaking her head with sympathy.

She turns the pages, carefully placing each one face down, after it is read. Renee falls asleep on her lap and Kathryn climbs onto mine.

Phuntsho Wangmo reads my account of the conversation with Karma Yangki and her about childbirth and our mutual misconceptions. The noisy maid and her twelve-hour labour, Karma Yangki's two-hour labours and my drug-filled labour.

'Is that right?' I ask anxiously.

She nods wordlessly and keeps reading.

She gets to the part about Karma Chokyi being courted by Dr Thinley and her body language changes. She gently shifts Renee off one leg.

'I don't know about this,' she says. 'It might be embarrassing for Karma Chokyi . . .'

'I'll show it to her,' I promise.

'Mmm.' Phuntsho Wangmo puts the papers down. She still has a few chapters to go but it is after 10 pm and she is exhausted. She has been working day and night on the premieres, and her job isn't over yet.

She asks if she can take the rest of the chapters home to read in the morning. Mal and I will be going into the office tomorrow and she will let me know then what she thinks.

Her face and tone give nothing away. She just looks very tired.

It's a long twelve hours till I see her again, and when I do she is at her desk surrounded by chaos. The film is due to open in a few hours at the Lugor Cinema for two weeks of screenings but the sound check wasn't good.

The telephone rings constantly with people pestering her for free tickets. One cast member who asked for two free tickets suddenly says he needs ten, but all the seats have been allocated. This is no time to be bothering her with anything that isn't about the film.

Just before lunch, Kathryn is ready for a nap so Wesel Wangmo and I take her upstairs to sleep on Phuntsho Wangmo's bed.

I'm in luck. Phuntsho Wangmo appears at the door wanting to take a shower. It has been such a hectic morning that this is the first chance she has had. While she dresses in a fresh *kira*, deftly wrapping herself up like a mummy, she tells me she read the rest of the chapters over breakfast.

She says it was strange to see things that she thought were so ordinary and commonplace presented to her in a different light. She speaks slowly and, I suspect, is choosing her words carefully. It brought so much back to her about a very happy time, she says.

I ask if anything offended her.

'No,' she says mildly.

What about the rest of the family, would any of them be offended?

'Maybe Karma Chokyi.'

I promise again that I'll show her.

Wesel Wangmo, who is playing on the floor with Kathryn, is listening to every word but saying nothing. Phuntsho Wangmo pokes her with her foot. 'She says very nice things about you,' she teases.

And that's it. She is gone – back down the rickety stairs looking fresh and glamorous, to solve a few more problems.

I think that means it's okay, but I'm not really sure.

※

Today is turning out to be the hottest day of the year in Thimphu – a sweltering 29.5 degrees Celsius. Wesel Wangmo is still here. We keep saying goodbye to her but each day, just as she is about to leave, she cashes in her ticket and buys one for the following day.

Even in this heat the four sisters wear the full traditional ensemble: tightly belted *kira* over a *wonju*, with a *toego* over the top. They look elegant and stylish but underneath they must be roasting. I'm hot in a sleeveless shirt.

While the two elder sisters work in the office, Wesel Wangmo, Karma Chokyi and I take the children outside to play. We sit outside the hardware shop, along a low wall beside the footpath on the main street, as Phuntsho Wangmo's new 'maid', a young man, brings us tea. He is a family friend Phuntsho Wangmo brought back to Thimphu after a visit to the family's home village in the east. He is a wonderful cook and very keen. It's like a merry-go-round of maids – the maid Phuntso Wangmo used to have has moved up to Taba.

I ask Karma Chokyi if she would like to read what I have written about her. She nods and I hand over the chapters.

Kathryn is getting grumpy in the heat. She won't let me wipe her face clean and keeps tearing at her clothes, wanting to go nude. It doesn't help that her new sandals are chafing, causing blisters. We strip her down to just the bib and brace shorts. Delighted, she takes off, running and stumbling along the footpath, which fortunately comes to an abrupt halt at a wall. She stops and turns around again. Barefoot and with the remains of lunch on her face, she looks like a street urchin. Wesel Wangmo and I take it in turns to keep an eye on her. While the footpath is safe, the road is too close for comfort. This vigilance is exhausting and frustrating.

Both Wesel Wangmo and I are painfully aware of Karma Chokyi and the pages on her lap. Soon, Wesel is reading over Karma Chokyi's shoulder while I am trying to gauge her reactions from her facial expressions.

The new young maid from the Taba house cheerfully steps in and chases the giggling toddler for us. Kathryn discovers her shorts have pockets and spends a lot of time standing with her hands in them, grinning at the world. It's very cute and causes a pedestrian traffic jam as people stop to laugh at her.

Wesel Wangmo sits beside Karma Chokyi and takes the pages from her as she reads them. Two young men, whom I have not been introduced to, sit beside her, and it becomes a production line. As Karma Chokyi finishes a page she hands it to Wesel Wangmo who reads it and passes it on.

Karma Chokyi blushes and giggles as she reads of their first date – Dr Thinley arriving to take her for a drive, his hair combed and neat. She passes the page to Wesel Wangmo, who grins and elbows her.

'That is just what he was like,' she teases, and Karma Chokyi blushes some more.

It is an agonising hour or so. Finally Karma Chokyi is finished.

'Is it okay?' I ask.

She nods.

'I don't want to embarrass you . . .'

'It's okay,' she says.

Like Phuntsho Wangmo's her reaction is maddeningly understated. I persevere: 'I'll take it out if you would rather it didn't appear.'

'No, no. Leave it in,' she says. A group of her friends from school appear and she is caught up in the gossip of the day.

It isn't until that night that I know for sure that I haven't overstepped the mark and caused offence. Phuntsho Wangmo says she thinks it's fine. As long as Karma Chokyi is happy and I don't marry off all the sisters to Mani Dorji, then I have their blessing.

She says it with a big smile and finally I know it's all right.

16

Farewell

The film continues to be the talk of Thimphu and many people go to see it a second and third time.

The apple man (who, I'm sure, said he had no family), appears unannounced at a screening with his grand-niece proudly in tow. She is blind. At the end of the movie she said she was disappointed there wasn't more singing. The Bhutanese videos have been heavily influenced by Bollywood and always feature hours of singing and dancing. *Travellers & Magicians* is more European in style. It has Bhutanese music in the background but it is the dialogue and actors' expressions that drive the story. Being unable to read the English subtitles, and not understanding Dzongkha, she had no idea what was going on. Nevertheless, the young woman appeared pleased that her great-uncle Ap was in such an important movie.

One Thimphu businessman loved it so much he bought ten tickets for people who couldn't afford it and quietly handed them out.

They have a hit on their hands, and Phuntsho Wangmo makes plans to extend the season.

※

In the office over lunch is a rare moment to catch Mani Dorji, and I ask him how publication of the Dzongkha dictionary is progressing. He disappears into the labyrinth of rooms and reappears carrying a book the size – and weight – of several housebricks. It is a gift, he says.

I'm so excited. I was there at the birth of this historic tome and here it is, hefty and tangible in my hand. Mal sits beside me as we admire the cover. It says 'Advanced Dzongkha Dictionary' in Dzongkha script and English. With Mani Dorji watching us, we carefully open it. Except for that line on the cover, it is all in Dzongkha. All 1600 pages containing 32 000 words.

It seems obvious, now that I am looking at it, that it would be in Dzongkha. It's not an English translation of Dzongkha, it's a dictionary. I mean the Collins, Oxford and Webster dictionaries don't exactly feature any languages other than English. For some idiotic reason I was expecting to be able to read it, and of course I can't. Nevertheless it looks beautiful with all that elegant script and we turn the pages admiring it.

New words, I'm told, have been created for modern concepts. *Logrig* means 'computer', *gyanthong* is 'television', and *yongdrel* is 'internet'. Coming up with these words was a major challenge for the committe of experts. For example, in English, the word 'computer' refers to a machine that computes. But that was considered too vague as it also could refer to a TV. The committee decided that as computers work through programmed intelligence and are operated by electricity, the new word should incorporate both those meanings. Literally translated, *logrig* means 'an intelligent machine run by electricity'.

The dictionary probably weighs more than the rest of our

luggage but we don't care. It will take pride of place on our bookshelf at home. And you just never know when it might come in handy.

※

On our last night, the family invites us for a lavish farewell dinner at the Royal Thimphu Golf Club, on the edge of the city. It is a very elegant club, well known to Phuntsho Wangmo, who took a job there briefly on her return from working in the grand hotels of Austria.

The nine-hole course is quite spectacular, with its neat greens and weeping willow trees. It is situated above Trashi Chhoe Dzong, the magnificent gold-spired *dzong* that dominates the Thimphu Valley. It is surely one of the most beautiful places in the world to play golf – and enjoy a special dinner.

We have a huge private room to ourselves overlooking the green, with couches and a long low table where the buffet is served.

As we eat there are different conversations going on in Sharchop and English, and the children play happily around us. The mood is relaxed and easy. We feel so much a part of this family. I don't feel sad to be leaving, just extraordinarily privileged to have become part of their extended family. I've gained so much from seeing how they live and raise their children, and the unique, gentle approach to life that all the Bhutanese seem to share.

We will keep in touch by email and I know we will see them all again. Maybe Rinpoche will make another movie here or maybe Mal will need to work on his home and retreat centre in Paro. I'm not sure when or how, but I am sure that somehow we will be back. Didn't the shaman say that Kathryn would return again and again? Well, when she does, I'm coming too.

Mal takes a photo of the three mothers with the three girls on their laps. Then everyone piles in and the waiter takes one of us all.

Phuntsho Wangmo says that she is winding up her work at the hardware store. It is ready now for a manager to take over. And after she finishes tying up loose ends on the film, she and Renee will go to Phuntsoling to be with Tenzin. 'Tenzin is happy with the arrangement and I am looking forward to living together with my husband for good,' she tells me with a smile.

Wesel Wangmo has a ticket for the bus to India tomorrow afternoon and says she will definitely be on it. The time really has come for all of us to say goodbye.

We will go back to Sydney and our life there, though for how long is anyone's guess. Mal has film festivals to attend as *Travellers & Magicians* goes out into the world. Then he will be needed in India for the next stage of building in Bir. Kathryn and I will go with him when we can.

The girls fall asleep on the short drive home to Taba and we carry them to their beds. We have an early start. Karma Loday will be picking us up before dawn for the two-hour drive to Paro Airport.

Phuntsho Wangmo comes into our room as we pack and gives us some delicately woven place mats. Karma Yangki follows her with a new cotton *kira* for Kathryn, apologising that it isn't much. It is, of course, beautiful. She says she has more plans for changes to the house. It's not finished yet.

'I hope when you come back, my home is perfect,' she says shyly.

I tell her it already is.

Further reading

Babies
Robin Barker, *Baby Love*, revised edition, Pan Macmillan, Sydney, 2001.

Buddhism
Sogyal Rinpoche, *The Tibetan Book of Living and Dying*, revised edition, HarperSanFrancisco, San Francisco, 1992.

Bhutan
Stan Armington, *Lonely Planet Bhutan*, 2nd edition, Lonely Planet, Melbourne, 2000.
Barbara Crossette, *So Close to Heaven: The Vanishing Buddhist Kingdoms of the Himalayas*, Vintage Books, New York, 1995.

Websites
www.buntyavieson.com
www.travellersandmagicians.com
www.kuenselonline.com
www.siddharthasintent.org
www.rigpa.com.au
www.panmacmillan.com.au